57

TWANG WITH OUR MUSIC

Then twang with our sonnets,
  And twang with our dumps,
And heigho from our hearts
  As heavy as lead lumps.

                    Ralph Roister Doister

+5/-

5/-

4, WHITEHALL COURT, LONDON, S.W.1.

22ᵈ November 1943

You are too far off; petrol is too scarce; and I am too old. But you couldnt do better.

I heard the end of The Apostles and thought it came off magnificently. There is nothing like it in Gerontius; and now that the chorus has learnt it, I hope they will repeat it until it reaches its proper place.

G. B. S.

My wife died on the 12ᵗʰ Sept. last. Her end (at 86) was quite happy.

FROM G.B.S. TO THE AUTHOR

The first paragraph relates to one of the author's village play-productions which he thought G.B.S. would like to see; the second continues a discussion about the neglect of Elgar's *The Apostles*.

TWANG WITH OUR MUSIC

*being a set of variants to mark the
completion of thirty years' practice
in the uncertain science of music
criticism*

By

BASIL MAINE

With an Introduction by
SIR COMPTON MACKENZIE

LONDON : THE EPWORTH PRESS

THE EPWORTH PRESS
(FRANK H. CUMBERS)
23-25 City Road, London, E.C.1

MELBOURNE CAPE TOWN
NEW YORK TORONTO

PRINTED IN GREAT BRITAIN BY RICHARD CLAY AND COMPANY LTD
BUNGAY, SUFFOLK

Offered to the memory of a friend

SEE CHAPTER TEN

CONTENTS

ACKNOWLEDGEMENTS

Some of the material of this book has appeared in various journals and I am grateful to the Editors of the following for permission to reprint: *The BBC Quarterly, Musical Opinion*, The BBC Talks Department, *The Gramophone, The Eastern Daily Press*. Also to Mrs Carice Elgar Blake for permission to print the letters relating to her father.

B. M.

INTRODUCTION

BASIL MAINE was one of the enthusiasts to whom *The Gramophone*, the first number of which appeared in 1923, owed so much in its earlier days. Nor, let me add, does the gramophone itself owe a lighter debt. Nobody who reads *Twang With Our Music* will question the justice of that last remark.

I am grateful for the opportunity this gives to express my own thanks to the author of this modest, graceful and perspicacious book.

Anybody who knew Elgar will realize from the letters he wrote to the younger man that the great composer had faith in the ability of Basil Maine to carry out the task he had set himself. These letters recall for me the very tones of Elgar's voice. I hear him now saying over thirty years ago that Busoni's mind was the greatest in contemporary music.

Those who read the chapter about Busoni in these pages will understand why Elgar made that observation.

I was much interested by the confessions of musical innocence from Charles Morgan, Raymond Mortimer, Clive Bell, Roger Fry and Laurence Binyon, extracts from which the author has reprinted from old numbers of the *Journal of the British Music Society* when he was editing it. But indeed I have been much interested in every page of *Twang With Our Music* and I am sure that many others will be equally interested. Basil Maine enjoys the advantages of the professional critic with those of the amateur. It is a happy combination and it has produced a delightful book.

COMPTON MACKENZIE

LETTER TO A YOUNG CRITIC

Dear Simon,

I have just received your letter telling me you are on trial for two months as music critic for your local newspaper and asking for a few words of advice. I am glad the Editor is giving you this chance. As far as I remember, the newspaper in question caters for a good average intelligence, and, for a provincial publication, has a more than average circulation, although, as you say, only a small proportion of its readers are music followers.

In giving this counsel, let me think of you as typifying the younger critic, and address you in the third person. I hope I shall not sound too patronizing because to the younger critic I am wholly sympathetic, and if I have noticed (judging from his musical writings in the London Press) that he is sometimes intolerant and frequently humourless—that, in fact, he is apt to take himself too seriously and to assume that 'it' all began with him—I can well believe, looking back at my own beginnings, that these are the symptoms of growing pains.

Perhaps I may also express the hope that, in setting down this counsel, I am not giving the impression of being conscious of the approaching end of my own usefulness as a critic. Occasionally, in writing for the daily Press, I meet with a misunderstanding so unaccountable that discouragement creeps in like an unexpected fog. But, on the whole, my work as a critic, both in London, and latterly, here in Norfolk, has brought me many happy encounters through correspondence (sometimes through agreement, at other times through disagreement and friendly debate), and above all, some true and longstanding friendships with professional musicians, both performers and composers. In early days, I was conceited enough to think that one could not form a friendship with a professional artist and still retain the right to give a frank judgement of his work on a given occasion. I was not long in discovering my foolish mistake. The true musician is never afraid of candour.

But the critic must take care not to mistake candour for self-assertion—and that is my first piece of advice to the beginner. There is no virtue in frankness if it is the obvious outcome of prejudice and that little amount of knowledge which in every sphere of life is so mightily dangerous.

And the reference to knowledge brings me to this second point of advice: let him make his reading as comprehensive and balanced as possible. I know that circumstances often compel a young critic to enter his profession before he is properly equipped, and he must needs carry on his trade while still learning how it is done. In that case let him avoid pronouncing a judgement on an issue which he is unqualified to consider. Far better to concentrate upon some external, such as manner of performance, or the reaction of the audience; in short, far better to record some plain fact—far better, because it is not only more honest but also safer. Even if ninety-nine per cent of his readers are impressed by his exhibition of spurious knowingness, there is always the one reader who will see through it. And that is the reader the critic should always bear in mind.

Meanwhile, if the young writer on music is interested in a particular period or school or style, let him lose no time in studying that period as widely as possible, its general history, the trend of the sister arts during the same era, the social manners and conditions of the time and so on. The wider his horizon, the richer will his experience be, and, when all is said, a critic's quality is to be assessed not by the fluency of his pen, not by a talent for vivid reporting, not even by his great knowledge (though, to be sure, these things are not to be despised) but by his power to experience intensely and then to communicate that experience. Allowing for the characteristic overstatement, Bernard Shaw was not far out when he said that criticism written without personal feeling was not worth reading. If the critic is in an argumentative mood he will be inclined to retort that it all depends on the feeling and on the person, and certainly upon the person's knowledge and general culture. But there was a rough truth in Shaw's attitude especially when it led him to declare that the true critic will only be appeased by good performances.

Another point: the enemy of the good is the pretentious. That is, for the time being, my last word to the aspiring music critic. He should be endowed by nature with a nose for the genuine and the counterfeit. And let him take care to develop that faculty. To that end, I would advise him as far as possible to avoid discussing a particular concert with others in the audience, who may or may not be friends of the performers (I am thinking in terms of the provincial concert). Let him concentrate upon his own direct experience of the music and its interpretation and then hurry off and set it down while the experience is still his own.   There are always those who will lie in wait for him, hoping to impose their own experiences upon his, and if they succeed, it is certain that the focus of his thoughts will be lacking in clarity and a sharp edge.

If they fail, they will resort to other methods in an attempt to subvert the young critic's independence.   With the next occasion in view, they will play upon his dislike of unpopularity.

Not the least part of mastering his craft is to learn how to counter these wiles so that his readers may be persuaded that, however green in judgement, he is at least honest.

These, my dear Simon, are only preliminary hints.   I wish you well as you set out to relate the adventures of your young soul among the masterpieces, and I hope you will always be able to believe your ears.

Yours with a blessing,

Basil Maine.

ONE

Reconnoitre: Music Regained

THE ONLY figure I have seen as to the number of homes in the world which are equipped for wireless is 78,000,000; but that was several years ago, and the number now must be greatly increased. In itself, this condition of things would almost wholly account for the revolutionary social changes of our time. In Great Britain we have almost daily evidence of the extent and continuance of these changes. Though some are warning us that 'l'ère de la médiocrité en toute chose commence', it is equally possible to believe that this widening of the horizon will help forward the liberation of the human spirit. The effects of broadcasting on the individual, on family life, on social habits, on education, on religion, politics, entertainment, and sport, are everywhere apparent. But in no sphere of human activity have these effects been more completely transforming than in the world of music. Middle-aged people can well remember a time when an orchestral concert was, for the promoters, a risky speculation. Today every concert promoter of any experience can find his audience. There was a time, little more than a quarter of a century ago, when to listen to an evening of Bach would have been a misery for the average British citizen. That same citizen today goes to a Bach Promenade Concert and, with thousands of his fellows, cheers the music and the performers as though a victory had been won.

It *is* a victory, of course. To have widened the outlook and perception of this average man so that his range of experience includes the finer creations of music means the defeat of ignorance in a field which in this country has been long occupied by the enemy. Knowledge and sensitive apprehension of music were considered a necessary part of the education of the average German of the pre-1914 era. His opposite number in Britain at that time was ill-educated by comparison, and chiefly because he was so lacking in the appreciation of music. It had not always been so. Almost total though it was, it was only a temporary eclipse. Certainly it did not justify the publication by a German author of a foolish book about England called *The Land Without Music*. A proper knowledge of our history would have prevented the setting down of the preposterous judgements contained in that volume, especially a knowledge of that period when music was a factor in the life of the people and when no person was thought to be truly educated who could not take part in a madrigal or play a passage of instrumental music at sight. That period, much of the sixteenth century and the beginning of the seventeenth, was brief but of intense brilliance, and it has continually been a source of inspiration in the story of our native music. During those years the encouragement given to music by the Royal House was that of enthusiastic performers. Henry the Eighth exercised himself every day in playing recorder, flute, and virginals, as well as in composing. His daughters were keen musicians, especially Elizabeth, who was judged by Sir James Melville to be an excellent performer on the virginals. This impetus, together with the flowering of natural talent, produced an age in which music-making became increasingly widespread as a part of domestic life. Pepys gives a hint of its extent when, in his description of the Great Fire, he remarks that the river was full of boats taking in goods, and that hardly one boat in three 'that had the goods of a house in, but there was a pair of virginals in it'.

In some ways the patronage of music which has been consistently given by the BBC through the past thirty years and more of its history is comparable to that of the House of Tudor. It has been stimulating, educating, and beneficent. In the early stage there was the fear, indeed the danger, that broadcasting would create a nation of mere listeners and that amateur music-making would wilt and die. That danger has passed. After an intensive rediscovery of music, listeners have turned again to the sane and heart-warming activity of performing it for themselves. People have begun to sing and play again in their homes. Even more encouraging, they have begun again to sing and play in their local communities. Regional choral and orchestral societies are reviving in spite of the interruption of the war years. Moreover, whereas many of them used to be die-hard in their programme policy, an increasing number have become adventurous, some in presenting little-known or neglected works of the past, others in the performance of contemporary music. Perhaps the most hopeful sign of all, and the most persuasive evidence of the wholesome influence of broadcasting, is the advance of music-making in country districts and small out-of-the-way towns. For this, the pioneer and spade-digging work of the Rural Music School, first founded in Hertfordshire by Miss Mary Ibberson, has been largely responsible. More enthusiasm is required of country folk than of town dwellers to keep a choral society going. Distances are greater and often the work-day is longer. The enthusiasm has been found, however, and the achievement has been notable. Country folk are also beginning to learn once more how to play string and wind instruments, and from this, Church music is likely to profit again in the coming years. Those who have been directly responsible for the quickened interest in the performance of music in rural districts have not harvested these results without hard work, patience, and vision. But their work would have been even harder, and their patience more sorely tested, had they not been able to count upon broadcasting as an ally.

Broadcasting in Great Britain has been an equally stimulating factor in the revival of music in London and the larger provincial towns. Not so many years ago, radio was regarded with suspicion and apprehension by the concert-giving societies. They were haunted by fears which have since been proved to be wrong judgements, derived from a total misunderstanding of human nature. They believed that if renowned singers or players accepted broadcasting engagements, and carelessly scattered the munificence of their talents to nation-wide audiences, the public would gradually cease to value and honour their artistry and ultimately regard their performances as so many pennies from a machine-made heaven. The artists themselves had the same misgivings, especially the most eminent among them, and for a number of years one or two in America refused to have anything to do with radio. The same fundamental error was made about the music itself. Many concert-promoters were convinced that if people could hear the performance of a great work in their homes without trouble or preparation, nothing would persuade them to do anything so inconvenient and old-fashioned as to go to a concert.

We know now how wrong that forecast was. In recent years concerts have been better attended than at any time in the history of the concert-hall. The error was made because two things were forgotten : first, the social nature of man, which always urges him to assemble for an occasion with fellow-creatures of like mind and taste ; second, the irresistible lure of the magic of performance. It is true there are, in limited numbers, those for whom the sight of a soloist playing in a concerto is an intrusion which mars their full experience of the work as pure music. But these are not the ordinary men and women who form the majority of our audiences. Nor is the quest for this cold perfection of experience in music necessarily right-minded, for its logical end is the ignoring of the human medium without which the composer's images and thoughts could not be made to live again for us. Moreover, to withhold reverence for the act of performance itself is surely to miss one of the essential aspects of musical experience.

There is cause, then, for some satisfaction as we look back over the brief period which contains the story of British broadcasting in its relation to music. All the more when we recall that not always has the BBC been sure of its direction in this field. It is unnecessary to set down here all the wrong turnings the BBC has taken in the course of its young life. If four are mentioned, these will be enough to indicate the numerous and unsuspected pitfalls by which those who provide our broadcasting service are continually surrounded.

Decidedly, a wrong turning was taken when the producer of a radio play was first allowed to cut a slice from a recorded symphonic work and use it to introduce or round off or, least justifiable of all, to form a background to a scene or situation in the drama. This craze for fading music in only to fade it out again almost immediately, is one of the many symptoms of contemporary unrest; it also has the effect of increasing the unrest. With a whole library of recorded music at his disposal, the temptation for a producer is great. The fact remains that if the BBC permits him to continue being unscrupulous, not to say ruthless, in this matter, it is fast undoing all the work which it so carefully built up in the earlier years by means of its talks on the appreciation of music, and such an admirable sequence of programmes as 'The Foundations of Music'; for the keynote of all that educating system was insistence upon the organic nature of music and the superfine qualities of that nature. Besides all this, there is the question of the strong association of ideas which music induces. Where is the musical listener who, having first made fitful acquaintance with Ravel's *Introduction and Allegro* through the snippets which recur throughout *The Man Born to be King*, could listen to Ravel's composition in its entirety without finding it coloured (and quite wrongly) by the Passion Play? And where is the justification of this tyranny of ideas? The music-loving listener who also had a taste for radio drama, noting that some of the BBC's producers regarded a symphony as a thing of shreds and purple patches, as a mere item in the box of tricks manipulated by the effects department, could be forgiven for asking why they were given so free a hand.

Another doubtful policy was that which the BBC adopted some years ago when it followed the common fashion of measuring attainment by purely numerical standards. This was the phase when audiences were required to sit through a performance of *Titus Andronicus* merely because a repertory company craved for the satisfaction of being able to say that it had performed *all* the plays of Shakespeare. Expressed in a different form, it was the same mentality as that which led people years ago to keep a score-card of their attendances at *The Immortal Hour*. So, in a comparatively brief period, radio listeners were given, with no regard for their powers of assimilation and with no discrimination between good and pedestrian music, *all* the cantatas of Bach, every note of *The Forty-eight* within a fortnight, everything that could be unearthed of Scarlatti, Handel, Haydn, and Mozart. They were also given, besides innumerable experiments by insufficiently tried contemporary composers, stretches of Mahler and Bruckner, not because there was likely to be a demand here for their music, but rather as a form of penance by a few of our musicians who were conscience-stricken at the thought that when these composers were first being played on the Continent, they had been utterly neglected in Britain.

Opera is another field where it is difficult for broadcasting to find a path. When attention was turned to the standard operas and it was decided to use a narrator to guide the home listener through the mazy winding of their stories, a problem arose; for, if the narrator is to be of any use at all to one who cannot see the action, he must continually be at hand with descriptions and hints, and this means frequent and intolerable intrusion at the expense of the composer. However discreetly used, his voice is a distraction. No sooner has the listener surrendered himself to the illusion conjured up for him by the music and lost himself in its fantasy, than his well-meaning guide brings him down to earth and compels him to regard the whole thing from outside. This and other inherent problems appear to be almost insoluble, until the public is reconciled to fundamental changes in the aesthetics of the operatic art-form, changes which will undoubtedly be hastened when opera and television finally come to terms. At the moment it is difficult to believe that those terms will be to the advantage of opera as an art-form.

Since the days of its youth, opera has encouraged the heightened social atmosphere of the opera-house—the sense of occasion—and also, as to subject-matter, a close though not exclusive alliance with the exotic ; and in both respects, opera will have to exercise more than ordinary self-denial before it can become a suitable fireside guest. If ultimately a new art-form, called TV-Opera, is evolved, we can be reasonably sure that it will be the antithesis of what we have hitherto conceived as Grand Opera. Rather will it be a development of that *verismo* style of Puccini which has been freely drawn upon by Menotti. Meanwhile we can look forward to a battle royal between television and opera as interesting as that which has sometimes taken place between an opera composer and his librettist, as absorbing, say, as were the tussles between Strauss and Hofmannsthal; and we shall no more expect opera to have things all its own way than did Strauss in his drawn-out duels with his exacting collaborator.

Another policy which has been a cause of controversy (and these four problems will suffice to indicate how dark and thorny a forest the early pioneers of radio were entering) is that which is concerned with the building up of listeners' appreciation of music. For several years two distinct lines were followed in broadcast talks on music. There were the broadcasters who prepared listeners for a concert or a series of performances by dissecting the music to be performed and discoursing upon its anatomy; and there were those (and none since has approached Sir Walford Davies's virtuosity in this kind of talk) who would expound a Beethoven sonata as a parable, a musical story with an artistically moral meaning. This was the very thing for the type of listener who immerses himself in music and lies in it as in a warm bath, but it was unhelpful to the listener who likes to enter a symphony as though it is a wide sea before him, demanding action from him if he is to keep his head above the waves. The audiences which now consistently fill our concert-halls include both these types of listener as well as many other types. It can be assumed, therefore, that both kinds of appreciation talks have made their contribution to the building up of this public. But in the case of Sir Walford

Davies, it is clear that success depended chiefly upon the magnetism of his evangelizing personality. Whenever his free-and-easy, optimistic approach to music has been adopted by other broad-casters, less learned and less reverent, the result has been de-plorable, especially when, in the name of broad British humour, the music-talk has been disguised as a kind of two-named music-hall act. There have been times when the BBC has mistakenly taken the view that this is the only possible method of approach to music and to the potential public for music. It has not in-variably recognized the widely different classes of listener which are to be found in the average concert audience, and that the same method of preparation cannot possibly appeal to all these classes. The present writer took part for a considerable time in the BBC's appreciation drive, and when preparing a series of talks, was never happy in the knowledge that in presenting a symphony or concerto to those among his listeners who were primarily interested in its technical structure, he would be neglecting those who, while listening to music, habitually substitute ideas or images for sounds.

Listener Research has helped the BBC to make a clearing through this particular wood. Even in a satirical item like Stephen Potter's 'How to Listen', it is possible to realize something of the complexity of the listening public, how whimsical are its tastes, how unreliable its attention. But various and capricious though the quality of this attention may be, one fact is solid enough to be foundational in future policy, namely, the extension of public appreciation and knowledge of music in Great Britain since the beginning of this century. The pleading would be too obvious which limited this remarkable development to the period covering the BBC's history. The fact that the closing years of the nineteenth century and the early years of the twentieth saw the beginning of Henry Wood's Promenade Concerts, and produced the greatest of Elgar's works as well as astonishingly forward-looking music from other British composers, was a sure sign that something was afoot. Nor, in the surprised satisfaction which fills us at the sight of our crowded concert-halls, must we omit to reckon the pro-longed privations of our life during and after the war years as a con-tributory influence. Even so, the impetus which broadcasting has given to the spread of the unique culture which music provides, can already be seen in perspective as one of the landmarks of the nation's social history. Figures do not constitute an entire proof, nor is the metropolis in all respects representative, yet the strength of this stimulus can be roughly gauged by comparing the seating capacity of the old Queen's Hall, where the Promenade Concerts used to be held, with that of their present home, the Royal Albert Hall. The Queen's Hall seated about 2,000 people, whereas the Albert Hall holds 8,000 and is still not large enough sometimes for a present-day Promenade Concert.

A true perspective is essential. If we would view the impact of broadcast music upon public taste in proportion, we must also include in the picture a wide range of miscellaneous features: not only the creation of Elgar's *Enigma Variations* and *Gerontius*, but also the appearance and establishment of hitherto unknown foreign composers (e.g. Debussy and Sibelius) in our programmes before radio arrived; not only the Henry Wood–Robert Newman enterprise which, unknowingly, was preparing for the BBC's advent, but also the exploratory work of men who were Wood's fore-runners, Hallé in Manchester, Grove and Manns at the Crystal Palace, and others; not only the steady influence of Sir Adrian Boult's integrity of musicianship, but also that of Sir Thomas Beecham's championing and unique venturesomeness; not only the educating work of the broadcast talk on 'The music you are now about to hear', but also the skill of such a writer as Ernest Newman, who week by week, for these many years, has been able to present in a journalistic manner the finest musical scholarship to a numerous following; not only the reform of concert-pro-gramme construction since the unwieldy programmes of the early Proms, but also the fact that those early programmes would not have been so unwieldy if the promoters had not had so much ground to cover after a period of stubborn prejudice, prejudice which, less than a hundred years ago, had precluded the first performance in England of many long-established works, and which, incidentally, enabled two members of an English orchestra to affirm, when first they rehearsed it, that they could not discover a single tune in the opening movement of Schubert's C major symphony.

It is when we set the dismal picture of music in England in the mid-nineteenth century beside the glories of the first Elizabethan age, the contemplative quietness of the English Fantasy of the succeeding years, and the inspired strength of Purcell's utterance, that we begin to realize the nature of that triumph which is

acclaimed night after night at our Promenade Concerts and elsewhere. The fastidious are annoyed by the incessant enthusiasm.
They say that the crowded audiences show no discrimination between one composition and another or between one performance
and another. They forget that these assemblies are concerned
with expressing, not the niceties of criticism, but overwhelming
relief at being delivered from the prison-darkness of musical
ignorance. It is not that these tireless applauders have experienced conversion, but rather that they have rediscovered
themselves. In effect they are asserting that tunes like *Searching
for lambs* and *The trees they do grow high* could not have come
from an unmusical people, and that, in fact, as Vaughan Williams
has claimed, at the basis of our musical life are a power of invention and a poetic impulse unsurpassed anywhere. We have
always needed someone to speak up for us as Vaughan Williams has
done here, as Dryden did for Purcell, as Peacham did for Byrd,
and, we may say, as the BBC has spoken up for us since the earliest
years of its history. The only fear is lest our broadcasting prescribers of appreciation should become too patronizing.

The existence of a selective Third Programme will relieve us of
this embarrassment as soon as the prescribers on that wave-length
learn not to assume omniscience in their listeners. On the other
hand, it is to be hoped that the Third Programme will not be over-
run by that kind of guide and policy-maker who so flaunts himself
that the music he is supposed to be interpreting is obscured.
Just as it can be said of a conductor that he is either intent on
giving a true account of the music or is concerned chiefly with
giving a most excellent account of himself, so it is with the
broadcasting guide to music.

The divisions in the BBC's service at the present time are
almost ideally suited to the various tastes of the vast, heterogeneous audience for music which it has done so much to build up.
Normally, the Home Service provides the staple fare which the
average concert-goer expects, the music of what is termed the
classical repertory, together with the best-liked contemporary
works and an occasional expedition into an unknown region. Side
by side with this is the Light Programme, into which the more
tolerant music-follower discriminatingly dips, realizing that lightness and artistic merit are not mutually exclusive in music any
more than in the other arts; realizing, too, that he would do well

to have some acquaintance with the heresies of music—Jazz, for example—the better to counter the arrogant claims made by the high priests of those interminable rites.

The several Regional programmes are admirably suited to the encouragement of local enterprise in music, and perhaps the hope may be expressed that the better sort of amateur endeavour will in future be more freely admitted, especially that which has been fostered by the Rural Music Schools. Everything is to be gained, too, by reinforcing the alliances between broadcasting and other organizations which provide for local demands for music and music-making, such as the Arts Council, the Workers' Educational Association, the Royal School of Church Music, the Rural Community Councils, and other movements.

There is this to be said for the Third Programme; it is solid evidence that the BBC has not helped to reclaim this great family of music-followers in our land without a sense of responsibility towards them. Of the Third it can be remarked without reserve that conscientiousness has been the hall-mark of all its work. Its services to music can be great. It can take up many threads which were left loosely hanging in 1939 when all long-term plans were cut short by war. For instance, it can continue to cultivate the ground broken by the 'Foundations of Music' series; indeed there are signs that this intensive culture is being increased. It can do much to help the rather more than average person to listen to broadcast music with a keener historical sense, to listen to a song by Dowland, a motet by Orlando Gibbons, a fantasy by Jenkins, a quartet by Haydn, or a nocturne by Field, with something of the same kind of associations and experience (as far as humanly possible) as those which the contemporaries of these several composers had. It can help to quicken that same listener's interest in the music of his own contemporaries; but in this case he must be sure that the music has first of all enlisted the genuine interest of those who have chosen it for broadcasting, and is not being paraded for the sake of notoriety or any of the ulterior reasons commonly associated with modernity. Above all, while other programmes are helping still further to increase audiences for all kinds of music, the Third can do much to refine the quality of attention of existing audiences. Especially can it keep alive and strengthen the conviction that, however great the advantages of listening to (or looking at) a concert at home, they can never outweigh the direct experience of the music in the concert-hall itself. Certain exceptions come to mind. An evening at the opera-house can be made a torment by the unpleasant quality of one of the solo voices or by a singer who insists upon the near-note. Obviously the home-listener has the advantage here, as he also had during a memorable Winter Promenade Concert when Handel's *Hallelujah* Organ Concerto was given with the orchestra playing at one pitch and the organ blazing merrily away at another.

Such lapses, however, do not affect the broad contention that music must be a direct experience to be fully satisfying. (Especially is this true of the more complex examples of orchestral music; as for a choral and orchestral work of the plan and dimensions, say, of Delius's *Mass of Life*, it is impossible to conceive it in terms of broadcast music.) No one knows this better than the keen and practised concert-goer who has had the misfortune to be overtaken by chronic illness and must needs for the remainder of his life listen to concerts by means of the radio-set. It is as though he were viewing the old familiar landscapes from the air—the well-loved features are ironed out and the feeling of being enfolded by them eludes him.[1] Tantalized, he feels the music always to be at one remove from immediate experience.

In the nature of things, this must always be so. He misses the atmosphere of the concert-hall, the interplay of communicated enthusiasms from moment to moment between himself and the performers and the rest of the audience. He misses direct contact with the particular interpretation which is being given of a work, for between him and that interpretation must intrude the controlling engineer with his continually shifting gradations of tone-quantity. He misses the magic of performance, that sweet influence, that grace which alone can save us from a robot world of music, a world in which all music is processed by physical science after being bled white by analysing talkers on appreciation.

The BBC, in my own opinion, has been alive to this danger and has always been careful to whet the listener's appetite for the direct experience of musical performance—for example, by sending its Symphony Orchestra on occasions to give concerts in the provinces. That is to its great credit. It is often said that the spread of musical culture has been one of the most important of

[1] This aspect of broadcast music has been treated at greater length in the author's book, *The BBC and its Audience* (Nelson).

the BBC's achievements. With that one may agree: certainly no
broadcasting enterprise has been more notable. It is also said that
in broadcasting, music suffers less than the other arts from the
fact that the listener is not actually in the presence of the exe-
cutants. I cannot wholly agree with that view, as the foregoing
argument shows. Nor, I hope and believe, is that view held by the
majority of those who are responsible for our broadcasting policy.
The result of this first phase of radio's alliance with music is that
increasing numbers of people are going into the concert-halls as
into a new world, a world of which they first had hints in listening
perhaps to a broadcast from London or one of the provincial
Festivals. These cannot have thought that the broadcast concert
was a complete experience. They could not be satisfied that they
knew Delius's Violin Concerto or Britten's *Serenade*, or whatever
it was that first pricked them into awareness, until they had met
the music in the flesh and blood of performance in the concert-
hall, any more than others could say that they knew a Shakespeare
play until they had seen it in the theatre.

In relation to chamber music, these views are naturally to be
modified. But they are not to be totally renounced, for the fact
still remains that the potency of the music's spell must always be
greatest in its actual presence and in the presence of its inter-
preters, whether the occasion is a recital of *lieder*, of string
quartets, or of pianoforte music. But clearly, where the scale is
smaller and the performers fewer, there is less chance of deflection
and contortion. Moreover, the absence of the allurement of
orchestral colour, or of the heightened emotional warmth which is
native to grand opera, enables the listener to attend more closely,
if he will, to the essence of the music, the quality and nature of its
thought; and since chamber music is uniquely intimate in its
diverse moods, in general it can lead the listener to a closer understanding of the composer's mind. Small though their numbers
may be, those who listen to the broadcasts of chamber music are
among the most musical or potentially musical of all the BBC's
audience, and if the present enthusiasm in Britain for music and
music-making eventually bursts into the full flower of a renaissance, equalling in glory and more widespread in influence than
that of the Tudor age—and the promise is most fair—it is from the
quietly permeating influence of these few (sometimes derided as
'precious', whereas they are precious in the finest sense) that the

sustaining force will largely come, especially as they include a fair proportion of people who are competent at playing an instrument.

This progressive movement, then, is in reality the nation's re-discovery of the music which has always been latent in itself and which has been eloquently and creatively manifested in its former history. The movement was already in existence before the era of broadcasting. Twice it has been arrested and pushed back by war. Marvellously it has survived. One of the greatest blessings brought by the BBC to the nation is the part it has played in making that survival possible, and the stimulus it has given to the continued growth of the movement. Unless it is disrupted a third time, whether by war or the lead-lump fear of war, it is possible that it may prove more important than all previous phases in our musical history. In that event, we may appropriately adapt for use at Broadcasting House, the broadsheet to be seen at the entrance of many printing-offices, and claim that 'from this place' music flies abroad not to perish as waves of sound, but to en-gender itself, and that for thirty years and more this house has sounded the incessant trumpet of enlightenment.

C

TWO

Ayres to the Lute

IN JULY of 1925 and for four or five summers after, I attended the earliest of the Dolmetsch Festivals at Haslemere, where for a time I was under the spell of Arnold Dolmetsch's passionate devotion to the music and instruments of the Golden Age. One of his great problems was to work out the technique of the lute. He studied it for years, and it was some time before he felt justified in announcing for public performance a Fantasy of John Dowland for that instrument. This, I remember, was at the third or fourth festival. It was an evening of extremely humid heat. The lute he was to play was lying on a table at the back of the platform, and as he was explaining the instrument to us in his inimitable manner, we thought we heard the noise of a string snapping. It was like Dolmetsch to be so concentrated on what, in uniquely broken English, he was expounding, that he did not hear what we thought we had heard. Soon after there was, unmistakably, another *dzing*, and at intervals two or three more, all unheard by Dolmetsch. When he had finished explaining, he went to the table, took up the lute, stared at it for a moment, then, with a cry of dismay, held it up with strings dangling for us to see. But he quickly recovered and, 'Never mind,' he said, 'you must come to hear the lute tomorrow. Tonight we play the viols.'

Arnold Dolmetsch had many strings to his formidable bow. He played the viols, the viola d'amore, the clavichord, harpsichord, and recorder. The difficulty about playing the lute works of Dowland was that the composer had left no published guide to the technical approach to his works and it was necessary to devise a new fingering. Arnold Dolmetsch devoted much time to the invention of this fingering and even more to its practice. When at length we heard him play a Fantasy for Lute by Dowland, it was by no means a perfect performance, but it did help us to realize the contrapuntal difficulties of the work and, incidentally, to admire the expert lute players of Dowland's time.

John Dowland was the greatest of the composers who are grouped under the description 'the Lutenist School'. Even judged by modern standards, his song-writing was outstanding. His songs and those by other composers of the School were written for lute accompaniment.

Strictly speaking, the term *lutenist* refers to the player. Kings and nobles of the land always had a lutenist in attendance, and even as late as the middle of the eighteenth century there is record of a lutenist being attached to the Chapel Royal of St James's. The Lutenist and Madrigal Schools together form one of the most brilliant phases in English musical history. Dowland's contribution was important. It is remarkable to find a musician living at the end of the sixteenth century and during the first quarter of the seventeenth writing a song like *I saw my lady weep*, which, without exaggeration, is one of the great songs of all time. In the British Museum and at Cambridge and Dublin his works can be studied in manuscript. They reveal him to be a composer of striking originality—so much so that, although he is one of a group, it is never very difficult to distinguish one of his works from those by Robert Jones, John Daniel, Philip Rosseter, Tobias Hume, or Thomas Morley. Finely expressive melody, bold harmonies, and sensitive rhythm characterize him. Moreover, his accompaniments are not mere milestones to measure the melodic line, but show a freedom of fancy which, considering the time in which he lived, is extraordinary. Robert Jones, compared with Dowland, is less subtle, less serious. Dowland wrote a number of light songs, but his general mood is melancholy. He himself played the lute with great skill—better, it was said, than anybody in Europe at the time. His virtuosity as a player was known throughout the Continent. As a composer he was less well known; perhaps because he was one of many, for it was hardly likely that his contemporaries would realize to what extent he developed the art of song-writing. When we of the present day hear his songs and are impressed by the fact that they are surprisingly modern in feeling, we can look wise and speculate with little risk; but that perception was hardly possible for the musicians of his own time.

Dowland published three books of *Songs or Ayres* and was the first to produce such a collection. His first book appeared in 1597 and was reprinted four times in sixteen years. The chief melody of these ayres was given to the top voice, and there we have the distinction between ayre and madrigal where all the voices are of equal importance. There were two ways of accompanying these songs. The solo part was attended either by three other voice

parts or by the same harmonies on the lute. Dowland concentrated on the type so intently that he brought it to a high pitch
of development. It is hardly an exaggeration to say that the songs
of the great German writers of the nineteenth century are in the
same genealogical table as these ayres of Dowland's.

Concerning Dowland's birthplace there is some doubt. One
source of evidence suggests that he was born at Westminster;
another encourages patriotic Irishmen to claim him as their own.
Irish or not, he was like a later Irish musician, Stanford, in his
desire to study abroad. Dowland travelled a great deal and from
time to time received tempting offers from various nobles to enter
their service. But he wished to go to Italy, there to study with Luca
Marenzio. He travelled to Venice and afterwards to Florence,
where he played before the Duke and received many favours. In
1598 he became lutenist to King Christian the Fourth of Denmark,
and in this appointment received a handsome salary. Three years
later an incident occurred which seems to point to the superiority
of English musical instruments at that time—the King of Denmark sent Dowland to England to buy some of these instruments,
for which he was willing to spend a handsome sum.

In any account of the Lutenist School, the name of Dowland
takes foremost place; but, besides those already named, the group
also includes Thomas Campian.[1] By profession Campian was a
physician who found himself continually drawn to practise the
arts. He wrote a treatise on counterpoint, but was more renowned
as poet than as composer. His attitude of mind can be guessed
from one of his verses which begins: 'Strive not yet for curious
ways. Concord pleaseth more the less 'tis strained'—good counsel
for composers of all times.

Rosseter and Campian together published a work which bears the
title: *A Book of Ayres, Set forth to be sung to the Lute, Orpherian
and base violl, to be sold at his house in Fleetstreet neere to the Gray-
hound, 1601.* Campian wrote the words of these forty-two songs

---

[1] Whereas Dowland's settings reflect the general sense of the words,
Campian's are only a vague counterpart to the whole poem. With
Campian the ayre is for amateur singing; with Dowland it is a professional
but not, as with Purcell, a virtuoso affair. To Dowland's lyricism, Purcell
adds the theatrical, e.g., the setting, like an actor's gesture, of the word
'drop' in 'The snakes drop, drop, drop' and, most remarkably, in *The
Blessed Virgin's Expostulation.* (Note in this last the intensely dramatic
call upon Gabriel, followed by the dejected 'he comes not'.)

and also the music of half of them, while Rosseter set the remaining twenty-one. These were among the first composers to publish solo songs with an independent part for the accompanying instrument. The work of Robert Jones cannot be ranked with that of the other members of the group so far as technique is concerned, but he was a famous composer. (He wrote the song *Farewell, dear love*, a snatch of which is sung during the kitchen scene in *Twelfth Night*.) He, too, published a book of ayres. At the same time a similar undertaking was being started by Caccini, but he was a year later than the others in publishing his work.

As for the lute itself, even as early as 1530 it had already acquired a printed literature, including books on technique. In a later book [2] the kinship between the viol and the lute is plain to read: 'When you are to set your fingers upon the strings, you must not grasp the neck of your viol, like a violin; but rather (as those that play on the lute) keep your thumb on the back of the neck, opposite to your forefinger; so as your hand may have liberty to remove up and down, as occasion shall require.'

That close relationship between lute and viol had previously been confirmed in a number of publications, one of which, dating from about 1488, states that in Italy and Spain the '*lyra* (*sive leutum*)' was usually played 'without the bow', but that the bow was used 'by the masters' for the accompaniment and decoration of songs and ballads. This also suggests that the rich accompaniments which are so essential a part of the work of our Elizabethan song-writers were the full flowering of a development which had been continuing for at least a century.

The earliest European types of lute were four-stringed, tuned in the same way as a gittern. (Lute and gittern differed in shape: in the former the back was convex and oval, but in the latter the back was flat with an inward curve on each side.) There is a well-known reference to both gittern and lute in Nicholas Udall's *Ralph Roister Doister* (*c.* 1552), where Dobinet Doughtie, complaining of his manifold duties in the service of his philandering master, says:

> *With every woman is he in some love's pang.*
> *Then up to our lute at midnight, twangledom twang,*

[2] Christopher Simpson's *The Division Viol* (1667).

Then twang with our sonnets and twang with our dumps,
And heigho from our heart, as heavy as lead lumps;

.   .   .   .   .

Anon to our gittern with thrumpledum, thrumpledum, thrum.

If Udall is to be trusted in his onomatopoeic sounds, one would say that the lute of his day was more nasal-toned than the gittern.

Even in the earliest years of the lute's history, the number of its strings had increased, and this increase continued until, by the seventeenth century, there were twenty-six and sometimes more strings, all ready to go out of tune at the slightest disturbance. A lute-player of that time, it used to be reckoned, would spend three-quarters of his life tuning his instrument.

The notation of the lute is full of difficulties for those who are familiar only with the staff notation or tonic sol-fa. The lines of the tablature do not form a stave but represent the strings of the instrument, and the signs indicate the 'fret' behind which the player must place his finger. When we bear in mind that some of the sixteenth-century instruments had either five or six pairs of strings, and a single string, as well as additional strings for the bass in some cases, we can appreciate the appalling difficulties of the technique, and can well understand how it came about that Katharina the Shrew ended her music lesson with that quick and decisive gesture:

I did but tell her she mistook her frets
And bowed her hand to teach her fingering,
When, with a most impatient, devilish spirit,
'Frets, call you these?' quoth she; 'I'll fume with them.'
And with that word she struck me on the head,
And through the instrument my pate made way.

The reader who, having more patience and perhaps a more tactful teacher than Katharina had, wishes to play, or to sing and play, some of the little masterpieces written by the Lutenists cannot do better than study them in Dr Fellowes's edition. To sing them to the lute, perhaps with the bass played by a viol da gamba, is to realize their true nature, which is too delicate for pianoforte accompaniment. If a lute is not available, the delight of these ayres can sometimes be captured with a guitar as the accompanying instrument, especially if the strings are of gut and not of wire (a guitar with wire strings is *déclassé*), and, again, especially when the player models himself upon such artists as Segovia and Julian Bream.

THREE

The English Madrigal

BEFORE THE English madrigal can be truly appraised, it is necessary to have heard and studied some of the best examples of the sixteenth-century Italian madrigal, especially those written by Monteverdi. This pioneering genius was born in 1567 and spent part of his life as court musician to the Duke of Mantua. At the age of forty-five he began to look for another post, and a year later bettered his position by accepting an appointment in Venice. From that time to his death, thirty years later, he became more and more renowned through his unceasing activities as a composer.

As with his countryman and part-namesake, Verdi, his creative powers grew wonderfully with his years. Toward the end of his life he wrote that opera called *The Return of Ulysses*,[1] which, when we consider the immaturity of opera's technique at that time, is so surprising an achievement. In reducing his rather complicated story to the dimensions of the opera-stage, he adopted the only possible method, which was to make the music follow the dramatic action as graphically as possible without ceasing to be music. As M. Romain Rolland writes: 'Monteverdi was typical of that great race of Latin artists who can always accommodate their genius to practical conditions.'

The striking feature of Monteverdi's work throughout his career is his unfailing instinct for combining innovation and tradition. His *Orfeo* is a shining example of a style (the Florentine) which first of all has been assimilated and afterwards transfigured. The progressive spirit is similarly at work in the madrigals, which were the product of the first part of his career.

The type of composition called 'madrigal' is Italian in origin. It was cultivated in Florence during the fourteenth century, when it usually consisted of a few short stanzas, each sung to the same music. Love poems were most often the text; occasionally there is a satirical touch. It was from Italy that we in England received the madrigal, and we took time to find a place for the visitor in our

[1] The same subject in a present-day setting has been used by the Swiss composer, Rolf Liebermann, for his pacifist opera, *Penelope*, which was given its *première* at the Salzburg Festival of 1954.

musical family. Rightly we may boast of *Sumer is icumen in*, which appears as early as the thirteenth century; but not until the transition from the sixteenth to the seventeenth century can we point definitely to an English school of madrigals.

On the other hand, the madrigal had been acquiring characteristics—we had better not say 'taking form'—for several years when Monteverdi began to compose. About the time of the publication of his first book of madrigals, there were notable Venetians and Neapolitans whose aim was to develop melody without sacrificing polyphonic richness; in other words, to effect a compromise between horizontal and perpendicular music, between a texture consisting of several melodies running along together and one in which a single melody was thrown into relief.

Some of these musicians influenced Monteverdi, especially Ingegneri, who did much to develop a declamatory style, Luca Marenzio, whose harmonies are full of dramatic feeling, and Don Gesualdo, Prince of Venosa, musician and murderer, whose audacities both in music and in life resulted from a love of extravagant gesture.

Some of the examples in Monteverdi's Fifth Book (Malipiero's edition) are especially interesting as showing how the road was taken towards the aria and cantata; but their chief claim to historical importance lies in the bold use of what was then regarded as discord. François Fétis has no hesitation in asserting that by these madrigals a new system of harmony was created. Another set is to be regarded as a connected dramatic action, in which the composer is already reaching out to a style which later will serve him for opera. Again, in the remarkable nine-part madrigal, *Questi vaghi*, Monteverdi's feeling for dramatic expression breaks through a type of composition which was not by nature intended for it.

But in the opinion of Dr Burney, it was not Monteverdi but Marenzio who brought the madrigal style 'to its highest degree of perfection by his great genius, and', he states in his *General History of Music*, 'he was the cause of that great passion for madrigals which became so prevalent among us when our own composers so happily contributed to the development of the form'.

Whether it is true or not that Marenzio alone was the cause of the passion, it is certain that the influence of the Italian madrigalists as a whole is one of the many examples where foreign music has stimulated our own composers to attain more highly than otherwise they would have done. During the same period, madrigals by Lasso, Arcadelt, and Willaert were sung in England and some of the words were translated into English. The result, direct or indirect, was that for the first thirty years of the seventeenth century there flourished in England a distinguished madrigal school. Before this time we meet with secular music from such composers as Fairfax, William Cornish, Richard Davy, and William Newark, and in the middle of the sixteenth century was written that fine example by Richard Edwards entitled *In going to my naked bed*. A few years later there is Thomas Whythorne. But in these works Italian influence is to be found. The school which flourished at the beginning of the seventeenth century not only developed a distinctly national style, but also can be described as a range of lofty individual attainments. It is only necessary to mention such names as Byrd, Morley, Weelkes, Tomkins, and Wilbye to declare the eminence of this school. Greatest of them all, perhaps, is John Wilbye. In such works as *Draw on, sweet night*, *Stay, Corydon, Happy, oh happy he*, and *Oft have I vowed*, we find madrigal writing at its best, not only in England, but in Europe. The variety of rhythm, the fineness of the lines, the surety of the style, make these works outstanding examples of the art of vocal composition. They are not period pieces, but inspirations beautifully realized.

There is another point. Even as far back as 1560 family performances of madrigals were given. Nicholas Young, a lay clerk of St Paul's Cathedral, did much to make the Italian madrigal popular in this country. He published some part-books under the title *Musica Transalpina*. He can also be said to have started the first madrigal society here. Indeed, Young was an important influence in the beginning of the English madrigal school. He called attention to the fact, one that needs especial emphasis in our own time, that, better than to talk about music, to enter into wordy critical arguments about it, better even, it may be, than to be endlessly writing music, is to perform it.

It does not in the least matter whether the performances are given by professionals or amateurs. In fact, amateur performances often contain an element of spontaneity which may possibly be missing from professional endeavour. Not the least important of the influences derived from the madrigal period in English musical history is that which leads amateurs to meet together and, as best they can, to sing or play, to give and take, in consort.

In England, the Italian madrigal vogue did not persuade us all at once. As usual, we were cautious. There was a delay of fifty years or so before we finally followed suit. No less remarkable than this lag was the rapidity with which this form of composition developed among us and its complete disappearance after it had been played out. While it was with us, it flourished exceedingly, in quantity, quality, and variety, and, it goes without saying, its treatment by English composers was almost always unique and original. In the history of English music, the madrigal period appears like a strange, migratory bird, which seemingly finds our climate congenial and then, after a few wonderful summers, suddenly, for no clear reason, ceases to visit us.

The art of music was at this time in its infant days. We are only on the threshold of the first developments of opera. The beginning of the important instrumental forms was still a hundred years distant. It is not easy always to carry historical perspective in mind where music is concerned. Not long ago, for instance, I listened to a broadcast of that remarkable anthem, *This is the record of John*, and it was with the shock of new surprise that I reminded myself that when Orlando Gibbons was a child, oratorio, opera, sonata, and symphony, as *forms* of the art of music, were unimagined. And yet at that time there was one particular art-form of music which has never since been excelled, music apt for voices, without accompaniment. Indeed, during the sixteenth century, to all intents and purposes there was only one way for a composer to express his deepest thoughts and ideas, namely, through unaccompanied vocal music; and since this period produced such giants as Palestrina, Monteverdi, di Lasso, Marenzio, and William Byrd, this particular vein was quickly worked out, whether in the motet, the anthem, the Mass, the English 'Service', or the madrigal. To quote the Civil War as the sole or chief cause of the hold-up in English music between the death of Gibbons and the coming of Purcell is to be over-simple. The real reason was that there had been so many men of genius or exceeding talent working at once in a field which, after all, was not unbounded. Gibbons was adventurer enough to extend the bounds in his verse-anthems with independent accompaniment. But the art-form known as the madrigal came quite suddenly to the end of its de-velopment. Wilbye's second set of madrigals was produced in 1609, and he lived for nearly thirty years after that date but, apparently, without writing anything beyond two short anthems. The same story can be told of Tomkins and of Weelkes. After the former had published his book of madrigals in 1622 he lived for thirty-four years without producing anything further of this kind; and the latter, as far as can be discovered, wrote only one important madrigal during the last twenty-three years of his life. Nor did Gibbons, apparently, write any more madrigals after he was thirty, although he lived another twelve years.

We may confidently say that the day of the madrigal was over in the first years of Charles the First's reign. Henry and William Lawes and Martin Pearson wrote secular works for voices, but were mostly preoccupied with bringing in instrumental accom-paniment. Blow, Purcell, and Boyce wrote hardly any un-accompanied secular music; and when we come to the glee at the end of the eighteenth century and the homophonic part-song of the nineteenth century, the inherent character of the madrigal has long been forgotten, as though it had never been born.

What is our life? asks the fine madrigal which Gibbons wrote to words (probably) by Raleigh. What was this life of theirs in outward form? In a house such as Hengrave—which we may hope will one day be purchased by some musical foundation, seeing that Wilbye was so closely associated with it as resident musician to the Kytson family—in such a house, the daily routine began early. Breakfast was round about 6.30, after which the men would engage in field-sports, the ladies in embroidery, or perhaps, some of them, in hawking.

Town life also began early. The House of Commons would assemble, for example, at 8 in the morning, which seems to rule out the possibility of an all-night sitting. The chief meal was dinner at noon or even earlier. The afternoon would be devoted to games, or walks in the garden or into the country. Tennis or bowls were the games, and the latter, at Hengrave at least, was sometimes played for small stakes, for in the accounts of that house is entered: 'Lost in play by my master at the bowls in Draps hall, 8*d*.' For wet days there were chess, backgammon, dice, and cards involving bigger sums than 8*d*.

Some would devote their time to playing the virginals and the lute and to singing. Supper was at 5.30, and from Thomas Morley we learn that after supper it was the custom for the hostess to deal out the part-books and invite her guests to join the family in singing madrigals. Or perhaps, if there were players in the company, they would make up a consort of viols. From the evidence of Morley and Henry Peacham, it has been too easily assumed, I think, that every educated lady and gentleman in the land was a first-class sight-reader. But even if that is too rosy a vision to take of life at the dawn of the seventeenth century, we can be reasonably sure that sight-reading was then a more common accomplishment than it is now.

Such was the daily routine at Hengrave when John Wilbye was resident musician there in the service of Sir Thomas Kytson. At first his room at Hengrave Hall was furnished with the bare necessities, but after being there about twenty years, 'Willbee's chamber' was made more comfortable by the addition of 'one table with twoe trestells', 'two longe playne formes to sett truncles on,' 'one curtayne of blewe and yelowe say for the windowe', and 'one chayre covered with grene cloth frenged with yelowe crewell'. Wilbye received no regular payment for his services, but he was frequently given a reward, one being a lease of land.

If we like, we may think of Wilbye in his chamber working at *Sweet honey-sucking bees* or *Draw on, sweet night*, and, having finished, taking it to Lady Kytson to be sung by the guests in the house. But though we may assume the skill in reading the manuscript at sight and in keeping the time and rhythm of the several parts, we know too little of their idea of tone and volume and blend to be able to re-create such a first performance in the mind's ear. Nor can we go further than guess at their feelings as they listened to themselves singing these morsels of wistfulness and longing. Did they feel as we do after hearing (still more after singing) a madrigal by John Wilbye—cleansed and healed by these strong, honest lines of melody, artfully set running one against the other to beget their precise counterpoints of accent and rhythm, and seeming to be freely independent, yet always concerned for the commonwealth of harmony?

Perhaps so; but possibly not to the same degree, certainly not in the same way that we appraise and are thankful for this art, this fresh air of the madrigal. For we perforce must regard all music earlier than our own time, and this is especially true of sixteenth-

and seventeenth-century music for voices, as a retreat from the harsh context of our mid-twentieth century life, a refuge from the mechanisms which have usurped the very identity of music, and the wailings and howlings, the blue near-notes and *glissando* noises which are the effect and, apparently, also the cause of the thing which its victims are pleased to call love.

FOUR

'Our Indispensable Eighteenth Century'

So ceased the rival crew, when Purcell came;
They sung no more, or only sung his fame:
Struck dumb, they all admired
The godlike man,
Alas, too soon retired,
As he too late began.

PROFESSIONAL MOURNER though Dryden appears to be here in this ode to Henry Purcell's memory, his voice does carry a note of personal admiration. 'The godlike man' may be too easy a phrase, but in the image of the rival crew being struck dumb is something of the poet's own feeling. Many others were moved to mourn Purcell's death in the stilted fashion of the time, and from the general chorus we may infer that something of the nature of the loss was realized. The writer of the Latin inscription on his memorial in Westminster Abbey comforts himself that the guest, now living with the heavenly powers, can still be made to live on earth through the power of his music; but for Nahum Tate 'the Joy, the Pride of Spring is Dead, the soul of Harmony is fled'. To another it seemed that such a one as Purcell was born once in a thousand years. He did not know how little he was exaggerating.

The period that followed Purcell's death has been so much used by foreign critics as evidence of England's lack of musical instinct, that it is almost a shock to discover one who opposes that heresy. He is M. Henri Dupré, and he writes: 'When King Charles the Second welcomed to his court musicians from France, Germany and Italy, England had already seen the rise of great composers, and the art of music had been honoured for centuries past. To sum up: this devotion to music was the fruit of a deeply rooted national tendency.' And these are his views on the succeeding period: 'Nonetheless, it cannot be denied that, owing to the effect of foreign influence, English music lost consciousness of itself during the eighteenth and early nineteenth centuries. Not that it did so entirely. The flood of foreign influences failed completely to extinguish the fires of art that had been kindled by earlier generations. There were a number of composers during this

period. They did not lack technical skill, but none of them was
inspired by the breath of genius. No composer of religious music
had the fervour of William Byrd or Orlando Gibbons; in the
dramatic style, none possessed Purcell's lyrical gifts; none had the
popular charm of Weelkes or the gift of expressing his own emotions adequately. . . . [The composers of this period] made an
honest attempt to keep their art alive when it was threatened with
total extinction after the soul of Purcell departed. But their
powers were not commensurate with their conscientiousness.
All the same, the part that they played was not utterly sterile;
they were preparing for the revival that we are witnessing today.'

I make this quotation from M. Dupré so that we may bask for a
moment in the warmth of a good report—a rare luxury for English
musicians where foreign criticism is concerned—and so that we
may be willing to believe that in English music the eighteenth
century was not so much a barren field as one lying fallow. That
the interval was so long is only partly explained by the drawing
away of the English public to cultivate foreign fields; another
reason is the intensive cultivation to which the native plot had been
subjected during the sixteenth and seventeenth centuries, and to
which I have already referred in the previous chapter. We must also
bear in mind the anti-musical influence of the social and political
life of the period. Music was no longer a grace, was no longer a
necessary part of a lady's or a gentleman's accomplishment.
There were other fashions.

But, as our friendly foreign critic reminds us, it is unjust to
pass over the accomplishments of such composers as Arne, Boyce,
Croft,[1] and Jeremiah Clarke merely because none of them was the
equal of Purcell. Nor is it for us to minimize the talent of any one
of them on account of his unsympathetic attitude toward his great
predecessor. Boyce, it is true, revealed how seriously he misunderstood Purcell in his editing of some of the latter's Church music;
and Arne, in a letter to Garrick, shows himself to be either envious
or a poor critic in declaring Purcell's theatre music to be too
'churchy'. Still, when we reflect upon the misunderstandings that
we of today harbour in respect of the distinguished composers
whose careers have lately ended, we may well hesitate before
throwing stones at either Arne or Boyce for this particular reason.

[1] Croft's *Burial Service* is a small masterpiece of English Church music.

We are better advised to make what we can of their own contributions to English composition.

Thomas Augustine Arne had one of those early careers of which the English especially love to read. It was a time of conflict between the claims of music and those of the Law, and also between himself and his father. In the end the parent decided to allow his son's natural talent to develop. How often we encounter such instances and how warm is our interest in these recordings! We are flattered, of course, by the fact that an English boy should be accidentally endowed with a musical gift, but even more, I suspect, by the blunt good sense which the male parent commonly displays in the crisis by setting his face against a musical career.[2] It is an implicit assurance that Britannia, however willingly she may patronize the art of music, will never become emasculated.

The opposition which young Arne faced provides a norm for the period in which he lived. It would have been a fantastic thing indeed had he been encouraged to follow a career in music. How much despised the profession was is reflected in the literature of these years, which was not so much a sister art as a distant and disdainful cousin. Addison had good reason to be distant, for he had written the libretto for Thomas Clayton's opera *Rosamond*, which was a ridiculous failure. Other writers were distant because of a lack of any kind of interest in music except as a subject for satire.

If it pleases us, we may play with the opinion that, had Arne been a greater composer of opera than he was, Handel's conquest of London would not have been so complete, for all that *Rinaldo* was staged only a year after Arne's birth. None the less, the fact that a man's career can demand visible recognition even after the bicentenary of his birth has gone by, points to some endearing quality in his work. In 1952, for example, Thomas Arne's memory was honoured by the unveiling of a tablet in St Paul's Church, Covent Garden. Furthermore, the Trinity College of Music, celebrating its jubilee that year, began to subscribe for two windows to adorn its building, one to Purcell, the other to John of Forncett, and these central figures were to be surrounded by small portraits of the most influential English musicians (both in sacred and secular music) of each century; and in this connexion, Thomas Arne was chosen as the most fitting representative of English secular music in the eighteenth century. These tributes are not to

[2] See also Chapter 10.

D

be taken to mean that Arne was a genius. Nothing in the whole range of his music justifies that title, whether we regard the overtures for orchestra, the organ concertos, or the harpsichord sonatas. None of his theatre music will bear comparison with Purcell's, a judgement which may seem ungrateful after the success of Sir Nigel Playfair's production of *Love in a Village*, in April 1928,[3] and of Arthur Oldham's version which was so enjoyable a production at the Aldeburgh Festival of 1954.[4] Apart from *Rule Britannia*, the Shakespeare songs will perpetuate Arne's memory more than any other of his compositions. But, frank, fresh, and free as many of these settings are, they do not catch the Elizabethan spirit as truly as some later composers have done. Unaffected and graceful, they yet miss the mingled tenderness and dignity and the warmth of heart which reside in these lyrics. They contrive to keep the sentiment of the words at a courteous distance.

It is always instructive to study a composer's work in the light of his contemporaries' opinions. In Arne's case, we cannot do better than call on Dr Charles Burney, for although he is loquacious, his talk is good and rarely fails to yield something to our advantage. Our learned host gives his opinion that an analysis of Arne's melody would perhaps reveal it to be a pleasing mixture of Italian, English, and Scots. Not only were many of his ballads imitations of the Scots style but in other songs (so Dr Burney thinks) he dropped into the same style, probably without intention. But Handel's style was not imitated by this English composer, even if he secretly admired Handel. Indeed, except in his essays in oratorio, Arne had no need of such a master, since he wrote for a quite different audience. Such was Burney's opinion. He also makes an interesting point about the poor fortune which attended the performance of Arne's oratorios. 'The oratorios he produced', writes this historian, 'were so unfortunate, that he was always a loser whenever they were performed. And yet it would be unjust to say that they did not merit a better fate; for though the choruses were much inferior in force to those of Handel, yet the airs were frequently admirable. But besides the great reputation of Handel with whom he had to contend, Arne was never able to have his

---

[3] But it must be admitted that only ten of the songs in that production were by Arne, and that the outstanding number, *My Dolly was the fairest thing*, was a melody by Handel.

[4] See *Festival Diary* in the Appendix.

music so well performed; as his competitor had always a more numerous and select band, a better organ, which he played himself, and better singers.'

In that passage we can discern the real problem that English music was then facing. There was foreign competition in the field. It did not begin with Handel. The vogue for Italian music and Italian performance had been growing since the year of Purcell's death. So much so that Thomas Clayton, of whom Dr Burney has the poorest opinion, deemed it advisable, in producing one of his operas [5] at Drury Lane in 1705, to make its substance as Italian as possible. Gradually, English singers were ousted by the Italian artists whose fantastic virtuosity is faintly echoed by such names as Nicolini, Senesino, and Farinelli. But until Handel arrived in London, Italian music was still only a fashion. The production of *Rinaldo* appears to have consolidated public opinion. In addition to the magnetism of skilful performance, Handel provided that of genuine musical expression.

The ground was ready for the seed. A new and very grand opera house, a novelty in the form of singers who were comparable to trapeze-artists in technique and daring, the personal popularity of the Italians, the snobbery and wealth of Society, all these were propitious to Handel's development here. He developed in such a way as to remove from English musical history the stigma of being subservient to an inflowing foreign force. For if it is true that Handel was the biggest factor in English musical life in the eighteenth century, it is equally true, though not always acknowledged, that English environment was the most important influence in his career. Many artists who were born in England have less claim to be called English than Handel. This is not a question for ingenious argument. It is not even necessary to thrust forward as evidence the composer's naturalization as a British subject. There is the solid evidence of the music itself and the hold it has long had on English people. Yet although no music is more familiar to the average twentieth-century Englishman than Handel's, over the composer himself, his personality and character, hangs a veil.

In this age of radio and dutiful appreciation, there are few who have not at least a nodding acquaintance with the general features of Mozart's character and Beethoven's and Wagner's, even if their

[5] *Arsinoe, Queen of Cyprus.*

source of information has been nothing more precise than the trademark of a music firm. But of the numbers of English people for whom Good Friday means *Messiah*, few have even the vaguest conception of Handel's personality. Nor is this a rebuke; for there is no certain way of forming a very definite impression of the man who played so important a role in directing the course of English music. Handel's biographers have found few absolute facts about his life. There are, of course, the contemporary portraits; but no one who bears in mind how misleading a postured painting of a person can be will be inclined to form a complete or even a general judgement from these alone. The majority of these portraits show Handel as a middle-aged man; but there is a miniature of him as a young man, showing him to have been good-looking. The print called *The Charming Brute* by Goupy throws a side-light. In this the composer is shown with a pig's head substituted for his own, and playing an organ. Around his feet is sufficient food for a banquet. Handel, it is true, was not abstemious; but there is not the slightest evidence that he was a heavy drinker. Both poverty and wealth were known to him; and if he must be judged extravagant, it was in his generosity to unfortunates whenever his position allowed it.

As for his religious aspirations, there is no reason to suppose they were abnormal. A general opinion is that those grandly inspired oratorios could not have been written without a profoundly religious motive. That is too facile an assumption. The relation between art and religion is not so simple a matter as that. More than a little of our well-favoured religious music was composed by men who were far from being religious in the accepted sense. With Handel, spiritual development seems to have followed an ordinary course. Its most devout phase coincided with his years of suffering and blindness.

His turning from secular to religious texts for his compositions has probably led to some of the later misconceptions of his total achievement. The last generation honoured him for his oratorios, we can almost say for one of his oratorios. His operas were regarded as being so many handfuls of wild oats the sowing of which he afterwards repented. I recall one of my earliest music lessons when my teacher, by no means a stupid woman, informed me that Handel was never truly inspired until he had renounced the theatre. She used to say 'the theatre' in a horrified tone, as who

should say 'the world, flesh, and Devil'. To her, Handel's turning
to oratorio was equivalent to finding his soul. Even fifty years ago
that view was current and was countenanced by so perceptive a
scholar as Parry, who said in one of his Oxford lectures: 'The
enormous mass of his [Handel's] operatic works in the Italian
style represent the taste of a purely capricious class in one of its
most capricious phases. And, although there is a lot of fine music
in them, the operas serve for little more than to point to an unpleasant moral, and had next to no influence at all on the general
development of style and occupy no place in the story of musical
evolution.'

These were strong words and, with all due respect, the last
sentence is untrue. For if Handel's operas have no place in the
story of musical evolution, then Handel himself has no place there.
When we compare his operas with his oratorios, we find no change
of style to indicate a change of heart. There was no sudden
transformation of the man's nature, no conversion.

The portrait by Kyte in the National Portrait Gallery shows
nothing to suggest that Handel was an intensely spiritual man.
Remove the wig and the period clothes and there remains a figure
which could be dressed as a credible Friar Tuck—a very shrewd
friar, one would infer from the subject's half-turned, steady look
at the artist. We have Burney's evidence that Handel was fat, and
in his movements ungainly. He also tells us that the composer's
countenance was 'full of fire and dignity'; that although his
manners and conversation were sometimes rough and impetu-
ous, he was entirely without ill-feeling; that even when he was
furious, his humorous sallies, aided by his broken English, 'were
extremely risible'.

One of Handel's outbursts deserves to be remembered as
being the only possible way to deal with a *prima donna* who is
putting on airs. The singer Cuzzoni has two claims to fame:
first, she was one of the finest opera artists of her time; second, she
gave poison to her husband. At a rehearsal of one of Handel's
operas, this remarkable woman took it upon herself to criticize a
song which occurred in her part. She would never sing it, she said.
Whereupon Handel seized her, shook her, and threatened to hurl
her out of the window if she dared to say another word against it.
Cuzzoni gave in and, moreover, made that particular song one of
her greatest successes.

Does not that incident help a little to explain how much the great man appealed to the English? Nevertheless, we should be wrong to think that his contemporaries regarded him as an Englishman or an English composer. Not till nearly a century after his death did we begin to claim Handel for our own, and then, curiously enough, the claim was strengthened by the fact that the Germans were spurning his music as being too English. We cannot deny that there is some truth in that judgement, especially when we are reminded that the chests of our choral singers have never expanded more proudly on behalf of English music than they do, year after year, for the singing of the choruses in *Messiah*.

Narrow and shallow as the stream of English music was running during part of the eighteenth century, the prospect is not wholly discouraging. We may take some comfort from the sight of that broad river called Handel flowing for the most part through an English environment, watering the land so that it became abundantly fruitful in after years. Chiefly through devotion to Handel we can show some of the finest choral bodies in the world, choralists who have made possible the creation of an unbroken succession of important English choral works throughout the first half of this present century. Some historians hold that we have no part or lot in Handel's glory, giving as their reasons that we first of all looked upon him as a diversion and a curiosity, that we were fickle in our patronage, that we made him bankrupt more than once, and that our controversies caused him distress and bitterness. If those reasons hold good, then similar ones can be given to prove that we have no share in the pride of Elgar's achievement. But we know that in his case, as well as in Handel's, obstacles were set up not so much by the general public as by the niggardly attitude of a few influential persons. It is true that to his English contemporaries Handel was a picturesque and exciting invader; if we think of the arrival of Diaghilev in England and the way he caught the public's imagination, we shall have some idea of the impression Handel made during the early part of his residence in London. His contemporaries were not to know, at least during the early years of his career, that his life and works were to become an integral part of English musical life, but a historian who does not discern that fact is hardly to be excused.

It was largely in the name of Handel that the musical festival tradition was built up in England; and how English a thing that is!

To appreciate the distinctive quality of that tradition one need only compare an English with an American music festival—say a Meeting of the Three Choirs at Worcester, England, with the annual festival at Worcester, Massachusetts. The older kind of English music festival is not merely an occasion for music-making. Music is its central purpose, but around that centre other customs and pursuits have gathered, enhancing it and increasing its accommodation. When we recall that the first Meeting of the three western cathedral choirs was in 1724, and that within the next half-century the festivals at Birmingham and Norwich were founded, we can appreciate the sentiment that has accumulated through the years. We can also understand why, in an age when sentiment is unfashionable, some of these festivals have been suspended and others are in a critical condition. Undoubtedly they call for reform in some respects. The amenities of mechanized music have persuaded many that they are anachronisms as unnecessarily large, draughty, and inconvenient as a four-square Georgian house. Others are equally certain that if these old festivals are allowed to lapse, something precious and even essential will pass from English musical life.

If we grant that the festival tradition is an essential part of the English tradition, we must also grant that Handel's music has been an essential factor in the building up of those festivals. In the year of Handel's death (1759) *Messiah* was performed at the Hereford Meeting, and only of late has its position as an annual fixture been challenged. The hold this oratorio has had over the English people is an extraordinary phenomenon. However carefully we attempt to explain it away, the fact remains that no similar work has seriously rivalled it for over one hundred and fifty years. Some societies occasionally drop it in order to give a Lenten performance of *Parsifal*, but there is no real danger that *Messiah* will be supplanted by *Parsifal* as a Good Friday observance. For thousands and tens of thousands the chief item in that day's ritual is a performance of *Messiah*, either to take part in it or, if the voice is not what it was, proudly to follow it with the family vocal score in hand.

The tradition of performing Handel's music at the Three Choir Meetings began at the time when William Boyce was conductor.[6] This musician deserves to be singled out from the men whose work

[6] Boyce became conductor of this Festival in 1737.

forms the level background of the eighteenth century. As a choir-trainer and organist he was renowned in his day, and for his work as a composer was appointed to the Chapel Royal. He wrote both sacred and secular music and with sufficient professional skill and freshness of spirit to persuade a composer of our own time [7] to study and edit his work. Boyce fully deserves the compliment by reason of the merit of his music and also because he himself devoted much time to the collecting and editing of English cathedral music. This was a considerable undertaking, entailing the assembling of the single parts of services and anthems in use in the cathedrals. The result of this labour was a three-volumed work to which we owe the preservation of compositions by Gibbons, Purcell, and others. The collection was begun by Boyce's master, Maurice Greene, another composer who should be placed a little above his contemporary fellows, in spite of the flagrant faults which Dr Burney marked in his Church music. As for Burney's judgement of Boyce's achievement, it is sound and discerning enough to be accepted today with little qualification. 'Dr Boyce,' he writes, 'with all due reverence for the abilities of Handel, was one of the few of our Church composers who neither pillaged nor servilely imitated him. There is an original and sterling merit in his productions, founded as much on the study of our old masters, as on the best models of other countries, that gives his works a peculiar stamp and character of his own, for strength, for clearness and facility, without any mixtures of styles, or extraneous and heterogeneous ornaments.'

Burney himself takes an honourable place in this phase of English music. We should perhaps be the more impressed by his renowned *History* did the period not also include that other monument of historical research, the five volumes of Hawkins. Without wholly agreeing with Boswell's unfriendly opinion that Hawkins was solemnly inaccurate, and without denying the immense research underlying his *History*, we may prefer Burney's on account of the more direct experience of music which informs it. In any case, it is surely a remarkable tribute to the vitality of the writing that a new edition of the work should have been published in our own time. For all that he was writing it for twenty years and thinking about it for nearly half his life, Burney would have been astonished had some clairvoyant informed him that his *History*

[7] Constant Lambert.

would appear in 1935 in a new edition, with strange appendices—
lists of music recorded for a mechanical instrument, and with his
own numbering of manuscripts carefully checked and brought
up to date. He has well deserved this attention from a con-
scientious editor, for a return to his *History* never fails to stimulate.
Is it so serious a criticism, after all, that we, after the event, are
wiser (let us say, better informed) than Burney? It is true that the
English Tudor school receives unsympathetic treatment at his
hands; true, also, that he was all unknowing of the place that J. S.
Bach was to occupy nearly two centuries after his *History* appeared.
In his defence, we can only urge that few of his contemporaries
were any more discerning in these matters. Where Burney is so
enlightening is in his picture of the eighteenth-century world of
music, his first-hand knowledge (as a result of his travels) of out-of-
the-way incidents and occasions, and in his general criticism, much
of which can be applied to present-day conditions. Furthermore,
when, in 1776, he published the first volume, his avowed object
of filling up a chasm in English literature was indeed being
realized.

How much modern scholarship is indebted to Dr Burney has
appeared in several studies published in our generation. In his
Background for Domenico Scarlatti, as a single example, Mr
Sacheverell Sitwell frequently calls on Dr Burney, and always
returns with something very much to the point. We are especially
indebted to Burney for his affirmation of the influence of Spanish
popular music in Scarlatti's compositions; also for the reporting
of an observation made by the composer to Dr L'Augier, physician
and musical amateur. Scarlatti told this man 'that he was sensible
he had broken through all the rules of composition in his lessons;
but asked if his deviation from these rules offended the ear, and,
upon being answered in the negative, he said, that he thought there
was scarce any other rule worth the attention of a man of genius,
than that of not displeasing the only sense of which music is the
object'.

This, we may be sure, was also the opinion of Dr Charles
Burney, a man of knowledge and good sense, and an excellent
companion for all inquirers after the art of music and the manners
of making it. As for his good sense and good will, and his influence upon contemporaries, these are nowhere better illustrated
than in the correspondence which on one occasion passed between

him and Dr William Crotch. A quotation from this will make a fitting end to this excursion, for it will serve to illustrate the points I have been making, namely that this stretch of English musical history is not so forlorn as has been commonly supposed, and that a true record must take account not only of Handel, but also of the sensibility, appreciation, and intelligence of the representative English musicians of the time. It will also help, incidentally, to correct the view that the eighteenth century in England is typified by Gibbon's 'passionless impartiality'.

Dr Crotch [8] had been delivering various courses of lectures in Oxford and in London, and Dr Burney, being as good a European as Professor Dent has been in our own time, was concerned lest some of his opinions should be misunderstood by foreign critics. So, though a man of little leisure, he took the trouble to write to Dr Crotch a long letter in which this passage occurs: 'And now my dear Crotch, let me tell you for what friendly purpose I wished to write to you previous to receiving your last letter. It was to tell you that when I wrote you my congratulations on the success of your lectures, I had seen none but good-natured lovers of music whom you had delighted with your performances; but that after the departure of my letter I had seen some Germans and good judges of Music who have kept pace with the times, without being insensible to the merits of the old masters. These . . . are unwilling to subscribe to your severe and even contemptuous remarks on Haydn. They say that you oppose your opinion to that of all Europe, and at a time too, when all the musical world is lamenting his loss and singing Requiems to his soul. They say that your criticism will injure his fame in this country, and destroy the pleasure of the public.'

And towards the end of the letter he offers this excellent advice: 'Praise when you can, play the best productions of gifted men; and let alone the spots in the sun which are invisible to common eyes.' But Dr Crotch was a man of strong opinion and in a brave

[8] Dr William Crotch was born in Norwich in 1775 and died in 1847. His father, a master-carpenter, made for himself an organ, which his son William discovered at the age of two and upon which, so it is said, he managed to play a tune something like 'God Save the King'. Whether this is true or not, it is certain that at the age of four William Crotch gave daily performances on an organ in London, the instrument being at Mrs Hart's, a milliner in Piccadilly. Crotch became a man of many talents, for, besides his achievements as a composer, he had a great reputation as a lecturer and teacher, and was also highly skilled in drawing.

and courteous reply he wrote: 'There are admirers of Haydn who esteem him "not only the greatest composer of his age but of all ages". If his champions are offended that I cannot allow him the same degree of credit for his vocal as for his instrumental productions I am sorry. But surely *all* Europe is not against me? Will not Italy prefer the vocal melodies of Sacchini, Cimarosa and Paisiello to those of Haydn?' And in the same letter he sets down his opinion of Handel and, doing so, can be said to be speaking for numbers of his English contemporaries: 'You have been told that I idolize Handel, that I admire his works exclusively. No, my dear sir, I have praised him less than some would think he deserved. It is not for his Instrumental Chamber Music . . . it is not for his Organ fugues . . . nor is it for his Instrumental Concert Music . . . that I prefer Handel, but for the greatness of his mind, the accuracy of his judgement, the variety of his styles and his skill in adopting the thoughts of preceding and coeval composers.'

FIVE

The Essential Bach

THROUGH THE enterprise of Mendelssohn, there was unveiled at Leipzig on 23rd April 1843, a memorial to John Sebastian Bach. A description of the event appeared in Schumann's *Neue Zeitschrift für Musik*, including this interesting comment: 'Honour was paid not only to Bach but also to his sole surviving grandson, a man of eighty-four, still full of energy, with snow-white hair and expressive features. No one knew of his existence, not even Mendelssohn, who had lived so long in Berlin and, he supposed, had followed every trace of Bach he could discover. Yet his grandson had resided there for over forty years. No information was obtained regarding his circumstances, except that he had filled the office of Kapellmeister to the consort of King Friedrich Wilhelm III, and enjoys a pension which maintains him in comfort.'

This, and the fact that at the second centenary of Bach's birth the exact site of his grave was not known, gives some idea of the astonishing indifference to his music and his memory during the latter half of the eighteenth century and the beginning of the nineteenth.

The first centenary of his death marked a change of attitude, and the *Bachgesellschaft*, with Schumann as one of the sponsors, was begun in that year with a widely representative membership. There followed Carl Bitter's meritorious study of Bach, and a few years later, the gigantic study of Spitta, who, in striving to repair the former neglect, almost obliterated the composer once again with the thoroughness of his exposition. The gates of publication were now open. After the appearance of Spitta's volumes, John Sebastian Bach has become the subject of more books than any other composer, and both France and England have made notable contributions to the subject, France through Schweitzer and André Pirro, England through Hubert Parry, Tovey, Whittaker, and the fine work of Charles Sanford Terry.

Commensurate with the activities of scholars and publishers has been the consistency of public enthusiasm. The Bach nights at the Henry Wood Proms at the old Queen's Hall were a phenomenon of the London concert-world of the nineteen-thirties;

nor is the appeal of a Bach programme any less magnetic today, and during the bicentenary year of Bach's death we experienced some remarkable performances of his works with a public response which, to all appearances, was not so duty-bound as it had been for example during the overcrowded year of the Beethoven centenary.

Indeed, the present-day public is discovering that with the music of Bach, the appetite grows with what it feeds on. Not only in the great master-works, but also in the music of smaller scale, there is room for endless spiritual exploration, and through the amenities of broadcasting, increasing numbers of people are discovering in Bach's music a safe retreat from the strident urgency of contemporary life. This music, they find, is not an opiate, as that (say) of Delius so often proves to be; it is not a mere diversion, or a mere sensation, or a mere philosophy, or a mere exhibition of skill, as the work of this or that composer (the names come readily enough) is found to be after the fourth or fifth hearing. In Bach, the public is continuing to find an enduring art, something firmly founded and with a moral fibre in it. In the music of this unworldly Thuringian choirmaster, people are discovering, however unconsciously, something which they themselves have lost and are sorry to have lost. In his smallest fugue as well as in his great *Mass*, Bach gives us unfailingly the art of integrity.

His music is a reflection of his character as far as it is known to us. He seems not to have worried about public approbation. In all likelihood, ambition and fame never disturbed him. Genius, sometimes, is proud and overbearing. Bach's letters show no sign of fretful self-consciousness. They do reveal resolute purpose and the various qualities we infer when we use the word 'character'.

We of the twentieth century who feel that character in this sense is hard to come by, are irresistibly drawn to any manifestation of it we find, whether in statesmanship, the fine arts, or the art of living. In music it may be indefinable, but it is unmistakable. We find character in the music of Byrd, of Purcell, of Handel, of Beethoven, of Vaughan Williams, just as we do not find it in that highest sense in the music of some other composers of genius. In the music of John Sebastian Bach we find character in its noblest sense.

Compare the obscure life of Bach with that of the modish composer of our own time, living in an almost unbroken glare of

publicity and with fashion's hue and cry continually in his ears.
Given the qualities which were inherently his, Bach could realize
and contain his greatness without interruption from the outside
world. The life and conditions of our present time do not permit
the artist to develop any greatness there may be in him, unless he
contrives to withdraw from the world for considerable periods.

This greatness and moral strength in the character and music
of Bach, besides providing the musical public of the twentieth
century with an image of lost ideals, have also worked beneficially
upon those who have devoted their lives to the study of his life and
art. Certainly they are reflected in the scholarship of Sanford Terry,
both in his biography of Bach and in his study of the Cantata
texts. To underrate the qualities of this scholar's work because he
happens to be English, is false modesty. The clear organization of
the researches upon which his biography is based is the outcome
of unique knowledge inspired at every point by a single-minded
devotion. The object of the work is to make the life of Bach as real
as possible to the present-day reader, without pandering to the
taste for easy reading by including dubious pictorial details. In
most of the former biographies of Bach, too much space was
devoted to theories, too little to facts. This is true of Forkel's
monograph, of Hilgenfeldt's biography, and of Spitta's classic
work. (Spitta, of course, had the advantage of being brought up in
a parsonage where a strict Lutheranism prevailed, and so had a
sympathetic insight into Bach's environment, but his study
necessarily carries the blemishes of romantic idealization prevailing
in his day.)

In spite of Spitta's thorough research, Terry, through his
patient labours in Leipzig and Weimar among other places, was
able to bring some details of new evidence. In the first chapter,
where the Bach family is traced from Hans, a peasant living in
the Thuringian uplands in the early sixteenth century, there is
brought out the interesting point that, although music called
irresistibly to John Sebastian's ancestors, there was a marked
decline in the musical proficiency of his branch of the family just
before his arrival.

The great value of Terry's biography is that, at the close, we
feel we are taking leave of a musician (and a man) of courage,
true humility, and unswerving purpose.

Some time before Terry's biography of Bach appeared, he had

published his important work on the Cantata texts, and here it
may be said that his integrity has outrun even that of the composer himself, so much so that he seems to have landed in an un-
tenable position. Since it is a position in which the over-zealous
student is always in danger of finding himself, and since it concerns
the eternally vexed question of translation, it may be profitable to
discuss this work of Terry for a space.

How far must the translation of the text of a musical work be
literal, and how far must it be adapted to the needs of the musical
phrase? Terry is very definite in his procedure, and even if we
disagree with his decision, we can understand how it was made. His
hand was forced. He was faced with the tremendous task of trans-
lating over two hundred libretti, embodying every one of the Bach
Cantatas, and the various literary styles of Neumeister, Salomo
Franck, Christian Henrici (*Picander*), Johann F. Helbig, and
many others, mostly anonymous. Naturally, before embarking
upon this vast sea, Terry found it necessary to formulate a system
of immutable laws, lest there should be mutiny in his ship before
the end of the long and arduous voyage. The system is sum-
marized in these two sentences: (1) The translator 'must faith-
fully interpret Bach's often naïve *coloratura*'; and (2) 'Bach's de-
clamation must be held inviolable'. These rules seem simple
enough until we begin to apply them. Then it is we find that the
first rule is constantly running into exceptional cases where
enunciation is in sharp conflict with metre, and that the strict
observation of the second rule often involves an ungainly and even
absurd translation.

The opening of Cantata 104 is an example of this. The first
phrase, '*Du Hirte Israel*', is in three-four time, and is set to a
crotchet and three groups of triplets. The perfectly natural translation, 'Thou Shepherd of Israel', is ruled out because it involves
an alteration of Bach's phrasing. The word 'thou' is therefore
omitted. The result is reminiscent of the pointing of a psalm to
suit the rigid requirements of an Anglican chant.

But, of course, we must be wary of criticizing the musical
purist. His position is almost unassailable. He is the only man
who gives us assurance that the works of the great composers have
come down to us in their original form. We know too well what
tricks the musical editor can play upon us from our experience
of the various editions of Mozart and Beethoven, not to mention

the vocal music of the sixteenth and seventeenth centuries. The insertion of an ornament or the deletion of a phrase-mark by an editor can utterly defeat the composer's intentions; when these are ambiguous, it needs an exceedingly fine judgement to make a rightful decision. And when Terry is so meticulous as to object to the slightest deflection of a phrase, he is, *in theory*, perfectly justified. For the phrase is the very life-breath of music. Its character depends upon its inherent rhythm—that element which enables it to beget other sequential phrases, to be fruitful and multiply. And since the rhythm of the phrase is reproduced in the larger rhythm of the phrase-group, it follows that any slight alteration in the former will be magnified in the total effect, and thereby the essential style and instinct of the music will be temporarily obscured.

Yet it is possible for the musical purist to defeat his own end by an excess of self-denial; and when he is in dispute with the literary purist, it behoves him to resort to conference and a dignified compromise. Here are two lines from one of Terry's translations:

> *E'er gen'rous measure meeting,*
> *No more can God or man thee ask.*

Now these words may be the only English translation which can preserve the integrity of the musical phrase to which they are wedded, but there is always the question: 'Are they worth singing?' And this further question: 'If a better and more worthy translation could be devised, could it not be adopted without misrepresenting the composer's conception?' For it is possible for an editor to be more zealous in his guardianship of a musical work than the composer ever thought to be. Bach himself can provide many examples to illustrate this. There is in one of the earliest secular cantatas, *Was mir behagt* (written for a hunting-party), an aria, which is sung by Pales, the goddess of pastoral life. The accompaniment to this aria (which begins with the words '*Weil die wollenreichen Heerden*' [1]) is found again in its entirety in association with the well-known sacred song *Mein gläubiges Herze*[2] from the cantata, '*Also hat Gott*'.

If Bach allowed himself so wide a liberty as this—why should Terry restrict himself within the small confines of *coloratura*?

---

[1] 'Long as fleecy flocks shall wander.'
[2] 'Fond heart ever faithful.'

This small disagreement with the most eminent of English Bach scholars is made here only to bring out the point that, while it is good for a biographer to be imbued with the qualities of so upright a man as Bach, it is possible for zeal to exceed itself. Remembering Bach's great virtues, we must also remember that he was human. The sacred cantatas, for example, are better appreciated when we recall the circumstances in which they were written.

Indeed, it is not possible to appreciate them fully without an acquaintance with the form of service which was followed at St Thomas's Church, Leipzig, when Bach was Cantor there over two hundred years ago. Fortunately, we have one MS cantata, on a leaf of which Bach himself noted the complete order of service, and from this we are able to reconstruct the whole scene on one of those far-away Sundays in St Thomas's Church. The cantatas were an integral part of the service, and served to heighten the significance of the season or a devotional attitude expressed in the Collect, or an incident related in the Gospel for the day.

The Gospel for the fourth Sunday after the Epiphany, for example, gives an account of the stilling of the storm, and this incident is the theme for the whole service, for the motet at the beginning, for the hymns, the Collect, the sermon, and for the two cantatas which were written for that day. The early Lutheran services did not exclude the musical parts of the Roman Mass, that is the *Gloria*, the *Credo*, and the *Sanctus*. These parts, however, had no particular bearing on the day of the year, and gradually music was introduced with the purpose of underlining the character of each Sunday and festival day in the Church year.

About the middle of the seventeenth century we find the cantata used quite regularly for this purpose at Leipzig, and during Kuhnau's time (he was Bach's predecessor at the Leipzig church) St Thomas's had a whole set of cantatas for Sundays and Feast-days, and for weddings and funerals. For forty years, Bach turned out cantata after cantata, and, according to his son's evidence, he wrote five complete cycles, that is to say, just under three hundred cantatas. It is possible to go even further and to assume that over two hundred and fifty of these were written at Leipzig, that is in twenty-one years, and from this we deduce that Bach produced on an average one cantata a month during this period.

Working in this way, he had little leisure wherein to contemplate

E

any radical changes in the form of the cantata, so we are not surprised to find that most of the Church cantatas are built up on the same foundations and according to the same plans. Yet within these prescribed limits, Bach often brings about moments of great exaltation and fine expression. This is all the more to be wondered at when we realize what his duties were at Leipzig.

The boys and young men at St Thomas's School had to be trained to give performances of the music required for the church services. As Cantor, Bach's chief business was to train the boys to sing these services, to ensure their good behaviour, and to direct the musical part of the services. These duties extended also to the church of St Nicholas. A motet or a Church cantata was performed at St Thomas's Church on one Sunday, and at the church of St Nicholas on the next, and so on throughout the year, except on the more important Feast-days, when the cantata had to be sung in both churches.

The wonder is that, in the midst of this rigid routine, Bach should so often be visited by the inspired moment. In the cantata *God's time is best*, for example, there is an episode for alto and bass which, in conception, is of quite remarkable depth when it is remembered that Bach was little more than twenty years old when he wrote it; and, again, in the 27th Cantata there is a breath-taking transition between the fifth and sixth stanzas, the fifth being a farewell to earthly joys, a bass solo against a running counterpoint in the orchestral bass, and the sixth being a serene, unaccompanied chorale. It is the sudden breaking away from orchestral counterpoint which is so moving an effect here.

Such moments as these could only visit a musician who had been grounded in the doctrine of original sin, death, hell, damnation, and the devil. To Bach these ideas were real. Not that he was acquiescent.[3] The conception of Bach as a guardian of the Church and her ordinances and composing solely for the glory of God is derived from Carl Bitter, whose study of Bach appeared in 1865. This cultivated author, who was the Prussian Finance Minister, did a great service in presenting Bach wholly from the ecclesi-

[3] His resignation at Mülhausen, for instance, although primarily the result of the frustration of his musical development, was not unconnected with doctrinal controversy. Bach's genius, as reflected by his music, reveals a temper of mind which puts 'faith before formalism', as Sanford Terry points out.

astical point of view, but failed to appreciate the humanity of Bach, a humanity full of contradiction and conflict, a man and an artist fighting out from day to day of a busy life the issue between his duty to history and the pressures and new influences of his own age and environment. So it was that he missed the point that Bach was not merely expressing a religious atmosphere in his music, but was coming to grips with the old dogmatism, with which he had always been saturated, and expounding the complex problems of orthodox biblical interpretation. This was also Forkel's failure, but in his case the shortcoming is easier to understand, since Forkel was not an avowed believer. To call the music of Bach, as Forkel does, 'pious', 'devout', 'worthy', and to speak of the 'sacred style' of his organ works, is not to get very far towards an understanding.

It requires a sharing, or at least an uncommon penetration of the Lutheran outlook to enter fully into the art of Bach. An example of this was found in one of the early pioneers of the Bach movement, J. T. Mosevius, founder and conductor of the Breslau Song-Academy. Because of his deep Protestant faith, Mosevius was able to come to a more real understanding of Bach than Mendelssohn. He had heard Mendelssohn's performance of the *St Matthew Passion* in 1829—that performance which, together with Goethe's acknowledgement of Bach's greatness, was the true beginning of the veneration of the composer. A year later he himself performed it in Breslau. Thereafter he performed a series of the cantatas and wrote commentaries on these works. Through his influence, it can be said that Breslau was only second to Berlin as a centre of the rediscovery of Bach. Yet it was in this very city that Bach's music met with a fundamental misunderstanding, typical of the era. Two views, two schools of thought began to be formed. Whereas the one regarded Bach's music as the embodiment of the Evangelical tradition and sought to bring back his music, and Baroque music in general, to the Church services, the other, represented by Thibaut and Winterfeld, could not accept the cantatas and Passions as Church music at all. Winterfeld, indeed, although a great admirer of Bach, prevented the *St Matthew Passion* and the cantatas from being given in church. This was the generation that had broken away from orthodox religion and therefore was unable to penetrate the dogmatic profundities of Bach's art.

What of the storm-centre which is our own generation? Shall we at last discover, what has so far eluded all generations since 1750, the true essential Bach? Certainly his music is popular as it never has been before. But this very popularity, especially in alliance with radio performance and propaganda, may lead to a surfeit and a reaction. As Dr Colles reminded us, the future of Bach depends on a like-mindedness with him among present-day audiences. Such like-mindedness is especially hard for the public of this generation to attain. Where Bach was profound, we are shallow. Where his was a progressive, ever-creative growth, our lives are disintegrated. We will not say the easy thing by declaring that Bach was born out of due time. He was very much of his time, very much of history—the history of music and the history of religious faith. But he was, in his time, more than life-size. Life for him was an adventure of man's spirit, with the Christian faith its supreme expression. From his earliest years, his resolve was to be the servant of Christian music. When Mendelssohn was discovering him, he called the *St Matthew Passion* 'the greatest Christian music', but, being a true servant, Bach had no time to be conscious of supremacy. Music was the family trade. He therefore set out to master its many technical aspects. Whether he was providing music for the Court, or playing a parish church organ, or writing the Sunday cantata for the St Thomas's congregation, he was completely absorbed and single-minded. Like-mindedness is, indeed, a condition of the fullest understanding of this phenomenal art, but it is not so simple in our present distractions. Goethe knew some of the Chorale Preludes and keyboard music and he knew the secret of how they must be attended to. 'It was there in Berka,' he wrote, 'when my mind was in a state of perfect composure and free from external distractions, that I first obtained some idea of your grand master. I said to myself, it is as if the eternal harmony were conversing within itself as it may have done in the bosom of God before the creation of the world. So likewise did it move in my inmost soul and it seemed as if I neither possessed nor needed ears, nor any other sense—least of all the eyes.'

It is with something of Goethe's spirit that we must continue to approach Bach, whether in performing or listening, if we are to experience a full comprehension of his music. The way was pointed after the first World War by the younger generation of musicians in Germany, who in their performances revealed a sense of understanding responsibility towards the Master. The glamour of virtuosity and the vanity of personal interpretations they eschewed. To such austere musicians as these, the bloated orchestral transcriptions of Bach's organ works which began to be performed in America and England were travesties, profanities almost. We owe much to their influence and work, the authentic editions of Bach's works, the straightforward performances of the music, and the revival of the old instruments. The influence has made itself felt here in England in the formation of the various Bach Societies with the object of giving performances which shall be, above all else, authentic, and, as far as is humanly possible, 'like-minded'.

To attain this ideal two graces are required of us whether we perform the music or listen to it. The one is to be able to follow all the processes of Bach's musical mind. That is outward, and is not vouchsafed to all. The inner grace is that of positive Christian faith and Christian humility, which enables men and women who may or may not be greatly versed in the skill of music, to enter into the spirit of Bach's works as Goethe did in the words I have just quoted, or as Schweitzer did when, in the course of his discussion of Bach's counterpoint, he wrote: 'The tremendous power of his creative mind makes us tremble more than that of Kant or Hegel. His music is a phenomenon of the reality of the inconceivable as is the cosmos itself.'

SIX

The Candour of Mendelssohn

AN ENTERTAINING commentary on London life in 1829 is to be found in the letters which Mendelssohn wrote to his relations during a visit to England in that year. He was twenty then. He loved his 'dear London' and made several return visits to this country. But the strange English amused him as much as the society of Scotland amused Chopin. He was sure, for instance, that the English had no understanding of Shakespeare; at least, Kemble in *Hamlet* at Drury Lane gave him reason to think so. Perhaps we should have thought the same if we had attended a performance of *Hamlet* which ended with 'The rest is silence', and with Horatio immediately coming forward and announcing, 'Ladies and gentlemen, tomorrow night *The Devil's Elixir*'.

Two years later Mendelssohn was in Paris, where he took part in a concert which must have been almost as fantastic as Kemble playing Hamlet with one leg in yellow and the other in black. In the programme was a *Grande Polonaise* for six pianos, composed by Kalkbrenner. Mendelssohn was one of the pianists. The others were Kalkbrenner himself, Hiller, Osborne, Sowinski, and Chopin. What would we not give for a gramophone record of that assembly! Even more than we used to give for the sextet from *Lucia* in the gramophone's early days.

At the time when he was making the grand tour of Europe, Mendelssohn was a well-dressed, slim, short, good-looking, charming young man, with attractive manners and a slight stammer which for many people increased his charm. He was also well-to-do, being the son of Abraham Mendelssohn, the banker of Hamburg, later of Berlin. His grandfather was the well-known Moses Mendelssohn, whose *Phadon*, a dialogue on immortality (based on the *Phaedo* of Plato), had been translated into several languages. 'Formerly', Abraham Mendelssohn used to say, 'I was the son of my father, now I am the father of my son.'

In addition to the attractions already mentioned, Felix Mendelssohn was also blessed with an extra-fine musicianship, both as composer and pianist. Of Mendelssohn's playing of the piano we have several pen-pictures. Joachim was especially impressed by his staccato playing and by the combination of fire and delicacy in his performances. 'His chord playing', commented one of his pupils, 'was beautiful and based on a special theory of his own.' 'Though lightness of touch and a delicious liquid pearliness of tone were prominent characteristics' (this is the testimony of another pupil), 'yet his power in *fortes* was immense.' And Hiller, in a rhapsody of admiration which paid tribute to Mendelssohn's skill, certainty, power, rapidity of execution, and lovely, full tone, remarked that when he played, 'music streamed from him with all the fullness of his inborn genius'.

Of that natural genius we have plenty of evidence in Mendelssohn's music. It is essentially the music of youth, of fresh, clear impressions. Mendelssohn had no experience of being aged, or even of being middle-aged. The overture to *A Midsummer Night's Dream* was written when he was seventeen. It has been said, and it is fatally easy to repeat, that he never wrote anything better. What the critic usually means by this reckless declaration of opinion is that the music bowls him over by its spontaneity, its effortless fluency. Certainly, the orchestration is full of mastery, the form clear, and the invention sensitive and poetic. The rest of the incidental music for *A Midsummer Night's Dream* was completed in later years, but it embodied much of the material which the composer had invented in boyhood. (A similar instance is the use which Elgar made of some of the musical fancies of his boyhood in the music called *The Wand of Youth*.) As for the appropriateness of the music, it is a telling fact that many producers, even those who have a horror of being thought conventional, still choose it when they are staging *A Midsummer Night's Dream*. I well remember an open-air production at Oxford by Max Reinhardt, in which Mendelssohn's music was the conciliatory influence throughout.

The precision which contemporaries remarked in Mendelssohn's playing of the piano, is a no less remarkable factor in his music. It is very much in evidence in the *Dream* music of which I am especially fond of the *Nocturne* (the music played during the sleep scene in the wood), and it is apparent in everything Mendelssohn wrote. He believed that music was a medium of exact expression. 'Notes', he said, 'have as definite a meaning as words, perhaps even a more definite one.' The *Songs Without Words* are a logical result of this view. It is an opinion, of course, which can be seriously disputed, were we in a mind to debate the subject and grind our words down to the finest shades of meaning. But Mendelssohn meant what he said, even if he did not quite know what he exactly meant. No one who has ever heard the *Hebrides* Overture would ever doubt that. When Mendelssohn was travelling in Scotland he sent a letter home with the *Hebrides* theme written out, to show 'how extraordinarily the place affected me'. The theme, simple in the extreme, is unusually suggestive of a visual expression, a picture in the mind's eye of the curling and brisk breaking of wave after wave. The Overture, by the way, is admirably suited for a children's concert. It has both 'form' (sonata form) and a programme (it is music suggested by the coasts and seascapes of the Hebrides), and therefore can be made both enticing—most children look for pictures in music—and instructive. I am thinking of a city where a concert was given by the London Philharmonic to school children and where I was invited to visit some of the schools in order to give preliminary talks on the programme with the help of records. The *Hebrides* Overture proved one of the most popular items. Mendelssohn was greatly attracted by Scottish scenes and events. A visit to Holyrood Palace started him on his *Symphony in A minor*, a large-scale work bearing the unmistakable impress of the composer's mind. The symphony is played without a break, and the only important departure from classical procedure is the inclusion of a coda which is long enough to be regarded as a movement in itself.

Delightful, by reason of its light-hearted spontaneity, is the *Italian Symphony*. So smooth an accomplishment as this could be described as a happy marriage between the romantic heart and the practical mind.

Mendelssohn was one of those composers who are continually being stimulated by what they see around them. In his symphonies and his overtures this stimulation is obvious—in his chamber music, too. The beautiful scherzo of the Octet, for example, had as its motive a nature-picture to be found in Goethe's *Faust*. (The Octet, incidentally, is another impressive example of Mendelssohn's skill and knowledge at the age of seventeen.) When he discussed this subject of outside stimulation on one occasion, he said, in effect, that if Beethoven did not consider programme music beneath him (meaning the *Pastoral Symphony*), his followers need not be ashamed of writing it. But he was annoyed when Schumann went so far as to read sea monsters and magic castles into the *Melusina* Overture. Beethoven's idea that music is required not so much to depict the items of an inventory as to express emotion was more in keeping with Mendelssohn's intentions.

The Octet is not the sum of Mendelssohn's chamber music. The quintets, the six string quartets, and a pianoforte quartet (in B minor) have their happy moments, even if they do not absolutely satisfy the strictest requirements of those who, wise after several masterpieces, formulate ideas on the subject. For my part, I shall always regard the pianoforte trios (in D minor and C minor) with affection, for in Cambridge days I often took part in performing them and they formed a charming entrance to the galleries and rooms of intimate music. Even more intimate and homely are the *Songs Without Words*, which one day, I suppose, together with Field's Nocturnes will be rediscovered by pianists. (There was a time when Mendelssohn's name was as closely and exclusively associated with the *Songs Without Words* as Rachmaninov's was with the C sharp minor Prelude.) When pianists make this reclamation—and the G minor Concerto can also be recommended—perhaps some of our solo singers will begin to cultivate a few of Mendelssohn's songs *with* words, if only for the sake of their affecting melodies. And since I have fallen into the mood of pleading for some of the neglected music of this composer, perhaps a hint to organists may be added about the organ sonatas, which, unlike some sonatas for that instrument, can afford delight to the player without wearying the listener. It would be easy to say that the reason for this was that Mendelssohn enjoyed playing the organ, but so did many another organ-player who, none the less, failed to communicate his enjoyment in actual composition for the instrument. The reason, rather, was that Mendelssohn was through and through a stylist. He had neglected his violin-playing, but that did not prevent him writing an admirably violinistic work in his concerto for that instrument. The melodies of this lovely work, first performed in 1845, spring as freely as anything Mendelssohn had ever written, but they reveal a deepening of his nature. Melancholy more than tinges them; they are poignant. It was at this time that the composer had begun to be anxious about his health. His former exceptionally happy spirit was suffering a change.

In my own musical life, I cannot remember a time when

Mendelssohn was not *there*. In all music, in all talk about music, he was always *there*. My first coherent memory of music comes from the otherwise misty age of five or six: at the Norfolk and Norwich Triennial Musical Festival, in the St Andrew's Hall at Norwich, Albani and Muriel Foster singing 'I waited for the Lord' from *The Hymn of Praise*—I can see and hear them now! *The Hymn of Praise*, *St Paul*, and *Elijah* were then part of the English festival tradition. *Elijah* still is. When a progressive committee proposed to break the *Messiah* and *Elijah* convention at the Three Choirs Festival some years ago, they were soon put in their place by the sensible ones.

The choral writing in *Elijah* is one reason for its continued appeal to the English. Another reason is the dramatic quality of the music, a quality which has led more than one producer to deck out the work as an opera, a quality which has lured some of our choral conductors into dramatic readings which have had the effect of spot-lighting Mendelssohn's music and making it sound more theatrical than purely dramatic. I recall a performance, for instance, where there was no point of repose at the chorus, 'For He the Lord, our God', so that its breadth and dignity were lost—no point of repose at all, in fact, until the recitative: 'Though stricken, they have not grieved'. In a hustled performance of this kind, the urgency of expression needed for the chorus, 'Thanks be to God', is not felt. This is a climax which must be prepared by the most careful attention to emphasis and *tempi* in the preceding episodes.

Some of our solo singers have also fallen into bad habits in performing *Elijah*. Let the reader refer, if he will, to some of the earliest gramophone records of singers—of Andrew Black, of Edward Lloyd, of Patti, of Ada Crossley—and he will find that whatever the music, simple ballad or full-blown aria, these singers endow it with a spaciousness of style which is almost unknown today. Listen to Edward Lloyd singing 'Then shall the righteous shine' and note, not only the full quality of tone on the word 'shine', but also the beautiful sound *of the word itself*. Note also the art of breathing a phrase, the art of phrasing at its finest.

There was nothing fussy about these grand singers, no attempt to hoodwink the audience with vocal devices and effects. Their singing was genuine. The part of Elijah, of course, can be exploited by any singer who wants to thrust himself between

listener and composer. I have heard unpardonable things done
in the prophet's name. I have heard an Elijah who sang 'Call first
upon your God' with a suitable, challenging tone, then suddenly
shut off the full diapason to register 'I only remain' upon the *vox
humana*, as if to excite pity.

Singers are not the only people who entertain wrong notions
about *Elijah* and its composer. Critics, too, have been led into
saying foolish things on the subject. After a performance of
Elijah at one of the Hereford Meetings of the Three Choirs, I
went to have tea with Elgar at a house he had taken for the week.
We were just beginning tea on the lawn when Bernard Shaw and
Mrs Shaw arrived. Shaw was not long in starting a discussion.
'Of course,' he said, 'the trouble with Mendelssohn was that he
could not orchestrate.' (I used to be able to mimic Shaw's
'orchestrate'.)

'Now, I can't let that pass,' said Elgar, and he asked someone
to fetch the full score of *Elijah* from the house. This was brought
to him, and he called the company around him (his daughter and
niece, I remember, were there, and Harriet Cohen and Herbert
Sumsion) while he pointed out instance after instance of Mendelssohn's feeling for the right orchestral touch. Shaw subsided
and was grateful for the correction.

Mendelssohn's idea of the orchestra and how it should be used
did not permit him to appreciate some of his contemporaries.
This, in a letter to Moscheles, is what he thought of one of the
overtures of Berlioz, for example: 'With what you say of Berlioz's
overture (*Les Francs-Juges*) I thoroughly agree. It is a chaotic,
prosaic piece, and yet more humanly conceived than some of his
others. . . . His orchestration is such a frightful muddle, such an
incongruous mess, that one ought to wash one's hands after
handling one of his scores.'

Was Berlioz annoyed by such an opinion? Did it incite him to
score off his critic by retorting, 'Before handling one of Mendelssohn's works one ought to wear kid gloves!'? Was he em-
bittered? Apparently not, for he wrote to a friend: 'Mendelssohn's
talent is enormous, extraordinary, masterly, prodigious. I am not
open to a charge of partisanship in saying this, because he told me
frankly that he could not understand my music.'

I have yet to mention one of the most important of Mendelssohn's activities, the part he played in furthering the cult of

Bach. He was a leading spirit in promoting the *Bachgesell-schaft*. At the beginning of the nineteenth century, writers were already at work to correct the misconception of Bach as being an unintelligible musical arithmetician. Goethe's friend, Zelter, began to rehearse and perform some of the motets and at his house enthusiasts began to meet to study the several kinds of composition left by the master. Mendelssohn was one of this little group. Zelter was unable to appreciate the music of the cantatas and the Passions as much as some of the other works. So when the centenary of the first production of the *St Matthew Passion* was marked by a performance of the work (in 1829), it was conducted, not by Zelter, but by Mendelssohn, who had been rehearsing it with a small choir for two years. This performance made a remarkable impression upon the more intelligent music-lovers in Berlin. Four years later the *St John Passion* was given by the Berlin *Singakademie*, and two years after that, an abbreviated version of the B Minor Mass was performed.

When Mendelssohn came to England in 1829 and in 1832, his enthusiasm for Bach was an important factor in the directing of English taste. Part of the *St Matthew Passion* was performed at the Birmingham Festival of 1837 as a result of Mendelssohn's advocacy; and on 24th June 1844 Bach was included for the first time in one of the Philharmonic Society's programmes. The item was an Overture in D, and it was Mendelssohn who conducted it.

In his own letters and in those of his contemporaries are numerous glimpses which enable us to form a clear impression of Felix Mendelssohn; but none, I think, is more revealing than this, from a letter written by Berlioz from Italy: 'I have met Mendelssohn; . . . we speedily fraternized. He is an admirable fellow. . . . All that I have heard of his music has charmed me and I firmly believe that he is one of the greatest talents of the period. [Mendelssohn was then twenty-two.] He has been my cicerone, I called on him every morning, he played me a sonata of Beethoven's, we sang Gluck's *Armide*, then he took me to see all the famous ruins which, I admit, impressed me very little.' Then he adds a sentence which is equally applicable as a comment upon Mendelssohn's music: 'He is one of those candid souls one meets so rarely.'

SEVEN

The Pleasures of Innocence

SOME YEARS ago, when I was Editor of the *Journal of the British Music Society*, the idea came of inviting a number of people—literary critics, poets, painters, novelists, and so forth—who, without being particularly versed in music, were occasionally to be seen at concerts, to contribute articles on music from the outside point of view. Some of these contributors were my friends, and this, I blush to think when I now see their names, partly explains why they were willing, when I told them that the Society's funds were too low to permit a full rate of payment, to accept the sum of one guinea for a full-length article. Among the contributors were Charles Morgan, Roger Fry, Clive Bell, Raymond Mortimer, Tancred Borenius, and Laurence Binyon. I even persuaded the ballet dancer, Lydia Lopokova, now Lady Keynes, to write on the subject; and this, for an Editor as young as I was then, was something of a scoop, for it was the first article of any kind that she had ever written.

Looking back at some of these contributions again after so long a time, I am glad to find how much perception they reveal, and how helpful they are to the musician who wishes, without seeming to patronize, to share his experiences with his non-musical brother, or first or second cousin.

In those days, Charles Morgan was my near-neighbour in Chelsea. We often met, either in his flat in More's Garden or in my studio. Late one night, during the period when he was writing *The Fountain*, he called and asked me to improvise at the piano. At his suggestion I turned out the light, and drew back the curtains to let in the moonlight. I don't know how well or badly I played, but if (as is probable) I had at the back of my thoughts the Lorenzo–Jessica moonlit scene, I am relieved to think there was no idea of competing with the incomparable *Serenade to Music* of Vaughan Williams, for this happened long before that music was written.

It was about this time that I had the temerity to ask Charles Morgan to set down some random thoughts on music. Here is part of what he wrote:

It was with the sensation of being in a dream that I came to my desk this morning. If the editor of some scientific journal had asked me to contribute to his pages a treatise on mathematics, the dream could not have been more fantastic; for long ago, when I practised gunnery in His Majesty's ships, the calculus was not altogether strange to me, and I am proud to this day of my ability to add two columns of figures, as the fairytale says 'at a blow'. By stretching out my hand I could, if it were necessary, pull down from my shelves to aid me, several respectable works on mathematical subjects, and I dare say that, if I put a plagiaristic pen to it, I could write a tolerable obituary on my old enemies, x and y. But in all my library there is not one volume of which a musical critic would deign to flutter the pages unless it amused him to be reminded of the genuine enthusiasm of so unexpected a man as Mr Samuel Pepys, or, wandering yet farther afield, of the Aristotelian view of professional performers of music, so that he might on occasion correct their vanity by calling their attention to it. In truth, my books not only refuse to lighten, but positively frown upon, my present task. 'Here we are,' they seem to say, 'ready to supply your need when you turn to those matters upon which you are a little competent to write—to history, fiction, poetry or the drama. But music—what do you know of music?' 'Nothing more,' I answer, 'than a man may know of a woman he loves but has never captured.'

My ignorance of music is jealously guarded. Why? Not, let me assure you, because I am unaware that knowledge, if I possessed it, would give me refinements of pleasure which are now denied me; not because I do not respect, and sometimes greatly envy, my musical colleagues who make short work of my mysteries, and, if for a moment they are baffled, can ride off so splendidly on their Anglo-Italian horse; but because I had rather, if by the grace of God I may continue a child in any of the countries of the mind, be childlike in this musical country than in any other, for here I see God plain, and hear His voice, and feel His angels about me without questioning their wings. Anatole France writes, in one of those papers he contributed to *Le Temps*, of the attitude of children towards their toys, saying, very wisely, that their regard for them is, in essentials, a religious regard, a kind of fetishism; and he adds that, though religious, it is not spiritual, for 'spirituality is the supreme elegance of intelligence on the down grade'.

What was in his mind when he wrote this last definition, I do not pretend to know. Perhaps in its mental and unexpressed context it had for him a meaning more profound and less impish than any I can attribute to it in isolation. But the preliminary distinction which he makes between the religious and the spiritual is illuminating. A toy is a child's idol, surrounded as idols are by loves and fears and superstitions which are powerful because they are not reasonable; it is a being from another world and the origin of other-worldly imaginings; to this extent it is a religious emblem. But it does not inspire that feeling of the freeing of self from earthly association and of the dissolution of self, still living and at liberty, in another Being, which, to a mystic, is the first of spiritual apprehensions. Religion may be independent of reason, but is generally (Anatole France touches upon this point in speaking of idols and playthings) anthropomorphic in derivation, and is limited in its range by human needs and conscious and sub-conscious human desires. Spirituality is always independent of reason, owes nothing and indeed is repugnant to anthropomorphism, and is unlimited in its range. So at least I understand the two words.

Now my appreciation of music and my pleasure in it comes nearer than my appreciation of any other art to a sharing of the qualities which I have just attributed to spirituality. Music is, for me, unlimited in its range—that is, it may carry me I know not whither, towards God or devil, through imaginative countries that have no boundaries, no chart, no age. It is, for me, repugnant to anthropomorphism. I will go further and say that, unlike other arts, it has in my mind no relation to nature. Certainly my care for it is independent of reason, for I have not, and deliberately avoid, the musical knowledge from which musical reasoning might proceed.

This attitude has certain practical and highly inconvenient consequences, of which the chief is that I have extreme difficulty in hearing music in the circumstances in which it best pleases me. Every circumstance which lays emphasis upon the artificial or 'performing' element in the production of music is an impediment to my delight in it. Just as I should not wish, in Heaven, to hear the angels tuning their harps or to see the celestial conductor mopping his brow, so I wish, on earth, to forget the performers, the composer, the audience, and all else that insists upon music's human origins.

This was exactly the kind of thing I was looking for. The idea of publishing the series of articles was to illustrate the fundamental error of dividing humanity into two mutually exclusive groups, the musical and the non-musical. Music-followers, almost more than the followers of any other art, are always prone to regard themselves as belonging to a Masonic order. It is this attitude which the would-be music-follower has always found so forbidding, and which has driven him, in great numbers, to follow the several cults of jazz. To his uninitiated mind, Music, even more than Painting, is so much a thing of awe, that he is content merely to stand in the porch with bowed head. Those who are familiar with the pass-words and the mystic rites, and scarcely know what it is to be taken by surprise, can carelessly enter and, with heads erect, be thankful that they are not as other men are.

Many interpreted the contribution of Charles Margan as a rebuke to this habitual attitude. Especially did they welcome his correction of the musical public's excessive interest in performance. Many, of course, consider this view as unrealistic. Yet there have

been platform artists—Schnabel was one—who were always
striving to make their audience aware, not so much of the 'interpretation' (which is one of the jargon words our vogue-ridden
generation has invented for itself), as of the music itself. Such a
puristic attitude, of course, opens the gate to the *poseur*, but not so
widely as, every season, it is opened in the sacred name of interpretation.

Laurence Binyon was more reluctant than any of the others to
make his confession, but at length he sent me a charming essay,
from which I quote the beginning:

Yielding to friendly but firm pressure from the Editor, I have, with extraordinary rashness, engaged to write something about music from a
non-musical point of view. If ignorance of a subject makes one competent to write about it, I am unusually well equipped.

It always seems to me very odd and ill-arranged by nature that it is
possible to appreciate one art and not another. One would have thought
that the instinctive enjoyment of art was a faculty that would enable a
man to enjoy all the different kinds and manifestations of art. But it is
not so. We all know people who are madly fond of music and care
nothing about painting, say, and vice versa. As for myself, I have often
wondered if I should have grown really fond of music had I been
brought up in a musical atmosphere, and had ever so slight a training in
the appreciation of it. Probably I should; yet certainly, I had no instinctive craving for this special satisfaction of the senses. My family
were indifferent to all the arts, and as a boy I had to find out the joys and
meaning of poetry and of painting (almost their very existence) for myself. Instinct led me to my desire. But nothing led me to find out what
music was, or could be, to its votary: so I conclude that on this side
there was a grave defect in my composition. And it is remarkable that
poets, as a rule, are not really musical. There are great exceptions, of
course, like Milton, and in our own day, Robert Bridges. But Tennyson
is said to have only liked a brass band, and Swinburne is said to have
been unable to recognize 'God Save the King' when he heard it:
Charles Lamb (if one may count him among the poets) wrote ribald
verses parading his dislike of all music and all composers. It certainly
seems that the rhythm of language and the rhythm of pure sound are
not apprehended by the same faculty. Or is this not true, and is it merely
a lack of early training bringing about an atrophy by disuse? Or perhaps
a prejudice consolidated by habit?

In his conclusion Mr Binyon, like Mr Morgan, touches on the
intrusion of the performer:

There is another thing. In music the executant is so prominent that he
interposes a distraction. To one totally ignorant and inexperienced like
myself, the miraculous and quite superhuman accomplishments of the

performers on piano and violin are so fearfully fascinating that it is an effort to get past it to what they are performing. But for very shame I cannot continue this exposure of my outcast and deplorable condition before readers who are all in a state of grace. Let me hide my blushes behind the Editor who enticed from me these sad confessions.

On reading the essays again, I find much that is as stimulating as when I first received them. In Roger Fry's, which he called *Musical Confessions of an Outsider*, there is drawn an instructive parallel between what he calls the sentimental aura of a composition of music and that of a painting.

He opens thus:

There is nothing more flattering than to be asked one's opinion on a subject in which one has no competence, but which one would very much like to have mastered. So that the Editor's invitation to me to make a confession of my musical tastes and distastes and Mr Binyon's interesting essay on his, have persuaded me against my better judgement to execute myself.

It would be difficult to exaggerate my ignorance of music and my natural inaptitude for it. This is no piece of vain modesty, but a mere fact. In spite of that, I none the less somehow get from music almost, if not quite, as acute pleasure as I do from other arts where at least I know my way about with some confidence. Mine may therefore be a case instructive for the light it throws on how the non-musical approach music and what they can get out of it.

Later he continues:

I know from my long study of the art of painting how the constant application of one's sensibility to the works of various masters and periods gradually undermines one's native prejudices. One after another the great names justify their claims, and one becomes catholic in the end willy-nilly. . . . In music then I am narrow-minded. I take what comes to me easily and naturally and reject the greatest geniuses, even though I can recognize them as such, if they are not of my kind. What I think may be of interest for the study of aesthetics in this respect is the nature of these predilections to which I yield myself. Every work of art emits a certain sentimental aura, and a person may be highly sensitive to this without being able to penetrate behind it to the essential motive of the work. It is, I think, by the attraction or repulsion of this general sentimental tone that the outsider, however intelligent and sensitive, tends to judge the work, whereas those who can really associate themselves with its more fundamental qualities can become indifferent to such sentimental appeals. On that deeper plane to which those who really comprehend an art can attain, personal likes and dislikes lose their disturbing power and the judgement becomes far more objective and disinterested.

F

I believe then, that if I were not a painter or at least had not some intimate knowledge of the art, I should think Piero della Francesca superior to Raphael; I should prefer . . . Tintoretto to Velasquez, Millet to Courbet; I should hate Guido Reni and Andrea del Sarto like poison, and I might have a tender feeling for any artistic nullity whose emotional life I shared; all of which judgements actually appear to me erroneous.

There is then the sentimental aura peculiar to each artist, but even more powerful on the superficial amateur is the effect of the sentimental aura of a period. This, indeed, is the first preoccupation of the amateur. In architecture one man has a passion for Early Gothic, another loves the Baroque and derides the Early Renaissance. It is a world of partisanship and personal feeling which more or less completely disguises the essential qualities of the work of art.

What I suspect then is that my opinions on music will prove my general thesis. They will appear to those who really understand music of such a kind as the opinions on pictures which I cited above appear to me. They are, I suspect, opinions based mainly upon the general sentimental flavour, whether of artist or period. . . . It seems to me that in what I have heard of Palestrina I am no longer interested in the agreeable archaic flavour, but come into more direct contact with some profoundly significant creation. This sense of importance has nothing to do with the emotions of life sometimes aroused by music, since I get it far more from some fugue of Bach's or from some passages of the late Beethoven quartets than from more definitely dramatic and emotional music. At any rate, this sense of some important or significant idea in music is for me quite distinct from the pleasure of what I should call agreeable or charming music.

Bach, as I have already hinted, gives me in a high degree this sense of importance; indeed, he has been for a great part of my life by far the most sympathetic of all composers. My liking does not date from yesterday, but from those days when my more musical friends regarded him with something like contempt. That was when Wagner first dawned on England, and it was a real grief to me to be unable to share the enthusiasm of my generation. This, I think, was due to my limited understanding of music which prevented me from getting beneath the general sentimental tone of Wagner's operas. And this sentimental tone was and still remains for me entirely antipathetic. I never doubted Wagner's genius, but I hated too much his taste and his sentiments.

In more than one of these contributions an antipathy to Wagner is confessed. But Clive Bell, in this connexion, tells a story against himself. He had always detested Wagner—'the sentimental over-tones of his work, the melodrama, the heavy literature . . . the obvious nobility, the cheap iron'. And, not being a musician, he was totally unable to understand the one thing relevant, the music. This he was discussing one day with a younger friend, a musician, who remarked: 'You mustn't suppose that we like Wagner for the qualities that you dislike in him.'

'That remark', writes Clive Bell, 'threw a flood of light not only on my appreciation of music only, but on the whole question at issue between people of peculiar sensibility—sensibility which has been trained and developed of course—and people of general culture. And now, when I meet an intelligent and cultivated person who gets a genuine but mixed emotion from painting, who doesn't like Raphael because of his simpering Madonnas, or El Greco because of his appalling religiosity, or Chardin because his themes are commonplace, or Courbet because he is coarse and conceited, I murmur: "You mustn't suppose that I like these painters for the qualities that you dislike." '

Likes and dislikes were readily set down in Raymond Mortimer's declaration. Here was an uncomplicated account of how music affected him, of the behaviour of his mind in the presence of music, of his day-dreaming, and of his great enjoyment of opera, which he welcomed for its distractions. And in him was no violent reaction against Wagner. According to his own estimate, he seemed almost the least musical of all who were invited to make their confession. Yet, even though I suspected this to be an instance of unconscious modesty, it was curious to notice that his approach to music was instinctively right, notably in his willingness to enjoy music's structure for its own sake.

Here, for the final lively movement of these *Ignoro Variations* is part of what he wrote:

I know nothing about music. I do not even know what I like; at any rate, until I have heard it several times. I enjoy listening to music, but I doubt if I get one-fifth of the pleasure from it that musical people do. My memory for music and my capacity for attending to it are very weak, and I find the effort of attention intellectually exhausting. After a time I always give it up and fall into a dreamy or thoughtful state which the presence of the music helps to make enjoyable, and sometimes even profitable. I resemble most unmusical persons, I fancy, in my tendency to translate music I hear into other terms. Eighteenth-century music with its symmetry and repeated sequences often suggests to me very vividly elaborated versions, more magnificent than any that exist, of rococo buildings, successions of volutes rising above one another and silhouetted diagonally against the sky. Romantic music presents more frequently the images of dancers, while contemporary music seems to make a much more direct attack upon my senses. In so far as I have taste in music, it is not, I think, bad taste, which surprises me, as I know that those who have little feeling for visual art usually prefer bad works to good ones. Perhaps unconscious snobbery has something to do with this.

I particularly enjoy Mozart in his more melting or romantic moods, and a song like *Voi che sapete* seems to me to possess the same poignant quality as the Bargain Scene in *The Way of the World*, a quality that comes nearer to exciting tears than anything in deliberately tragic work. I enjoy opera greatly: the incidents engage my attention when I can no longer listen properly to the music. Wagner particularly excites me— I suppose it is the most literary sort of music. Almost every musical work seems to me too long: because my own attention is not long enough. I enjoy the material of music in itself: the mere tone of a voice or a fiddle, and above all the volume of a large orchestra give me intense pleasure. When I have heard a piece of music often, I enjoy the inevitability of the sequences of sound that compose it, and begin dimly to apprehend the pure emotion given by design which musical people enjoy.

EIGHT

Some Busoni Recollections

RETURNING from the International Festival of Music at Prague in 1925, I broke the journey at Dresden in order to attend the first performance of Busoni's *Doktor Faust*. I recall the occasion, not only because of the opera itself, but also because of two incidents.

Busoni had died in 1924, and this production was in the nature of a memorial performance. At the end, the whole audience rose and stood in silence as a tribute to the composer. In his admirable biography of Busoni, Edward Dent does not make clear whether he is referring to audience or critics when he remarks that *Doktor Faust* was received with respect rather than enthusiasm. If he is referring to the first-night audience, his remark loses point in view of the circumstance I have just mentioned.

The other incident occurred after I had left the opera-house. It was a fine, warm night, and without hat or coat I wandered alone through the streets, steeped in the experience which had just come upon me. I did not know Dresden at all, and soon I was quite lost. It was past midnight and I was far from my hotel, which was somewhere in the centre of the town. Moreover, I could neither remember its name nor the street in which it stood. I walked on for a while without meeting anyone: then a taxi appeared. My best plan, I thought, was to ask the driver to take me to some central spot and from there to walk in an attempt to find my hotel. 'The opera-house,' I said as casually as I could. The taxi-driver, I could see, did not know what to make of me, asking for the opera-house in the early hours of the morning.

Although I never met Busoni, I find he is prominent in the memories of the first months of my London life. Though the youngest of the music critics of the *Daily Telegraph*, I was occasionally rewarded with a plum, and several of Busoni's pianoforte recitals came my way, and are among the most treasured of my experiences of music. I recall, for example, the occasion at the Wigmore Hall when he played Beethoven's Opus 31, No. 2, and the impression that new ideas of interpretation were coming to him even as he played. At the same recital he played the *Goldberg Variations*, and all the time appeared to be wrestling with some

immense problem. There were moments in each of these performances when he was so preoccupied with details that for one
listener at least, the main development was temporarily obscured.
For all that, the lasting impression was of conviction carried
through sheer power and vision.

At another recital which I attended he played Bach, Beethoven,
Chopin, and Liszt, and of each composer gave so individual an
interpretation that his own name might well have been hyphenated
to each of the composers on the programme. It was always Bach–
Busoni that he gave us, and sometimes Busoni–Bach. As an interpreter he was so great as sometimes to be dangerous. He used
to remind me of that kind of great actor who, in spite of Shakespeare's own words, is able to convince us that Iago is not working
for Othello's ruin or that Malvolio is an heroic lover. I have heard
Busoni play Bach's *Chromatic Fantasy and Fugue* with marvellous
intellectual and technical strength, but also reading into the notes
a rich romantic emotion. His intellectual power sometimes led
him to make exaggerated, even grotesque, points of interpretation;
but one could always depend upon the performance being of the
creative order. Busoni was never content with mere technique.
Nor was he ever completely satisfied by the act of performing for
the public. There were times when I could really believe that he
had forgotten the audience, so remote and sublimely alone did he
appear while he played.

Of Ferruccio Busoni's life it was singularly true that the child
was father to the man. Most of the qualities that characterized him
in manhood were formed in early years. Already at the age of
eight the conflict between his Latin temperament and German
training was apparent. That conflict lasted all his life; and, while
it contributed to his power of profound interpretation as a pianist,
it was also partly the reason for the dark problems that clouded
his creative impulse. In a sense, creator and interpreter in him
were one. Especially when he played the later sonatas of Beethoven
did this become apparent. Another of his recitals comes to mind.
While he was playing Beethoven's Opus 111, I had the experience
of suddenly perceiving episodes, which before had been enigmatic,
in a clear steady light. It did not seem far-fetched to think of that
reading as an act of creation. In it there was something of the
same quality that is found in the *Fantasia Contrappuntistica*,
wherein Busoni took a fragment of a Bach fugue as the pretext for

a lengthy exposition. Philip Levi, one of Busoni's pupils, once played the work in London, and that was another experience. The exposition lasts for about half-an-hour, during which the composer makes use of all kinds of formal devices, choral prelude, fugue, intermezzo, variations, cadenza, chorale. All the time he piles up invention upon invention until the task of concentration becomes almost too heavy for one sitting. But at the moment when the material of the music seems about to defeat the conceiving mind, that mind suddenly takes command, marshals its forces, and by means of a movement of brilliant strategy, reaches its destination.

In Busoni's actual career one looks in vain for such a *stretto*. The elements of his most complex nature brought about a tragic conflict, which was carried out on the heroic plane. In a few words, the tragedy of Busoni's career was that he could never be satisfied that he had brought the best out of himself. (I mean in the sense that Elgar, having completed *Gerontius*, believed that he had given the best of himself.) *Doktor Faust* brought him nearest to that satisfaction. In that opera his purpose was not only to work out his theories but also to gather the fruits of his remarkable life. It was to be the summing-up of his life's work.

In many of Busoni's larger compositions there is a development of smaller works. *Doktor Faust*, for example, is an expansion of earlier ideas. The opera reveals how aloof was the composer's mind, how he strove to avoid any set, categorical style. In preparing the text, he discarded all the conventions of the Faust story, and based his work on the puppet-show version. The episode concerning the Countess of Parma becomes prominent. (In this, Faust practises necromancy before the Count and Countess on their wedding-night, and the Countess falls a victim to his power.) The close of the opera is far removed from the traditional descent into hell. Busoni's Faust reaches a metaphysical plane beyond all ideas of God and Devil, and is content to dwell in the consciousness of his own ego. This is to be continued after his death in the child-figure which a beggar-woman (the Countess of Parma) in a Wittenberg street has left with him. That child-figure becomes the symbol of the continuity of his own spirit.

Incidentally, the symbol of the child-figure possibly originated in Busoni's yearning for a childhood that had never been his. To read of young Ferruccio being dragged round Europe by his father is as moving as to recall the ardours of Mozart's boyhood. 'He [my father] considered me mature and marvellous enough'—these were Busoni's words—'to take me to Vienna as pianist, composer and improviser.' This refers to the year 1875, when Ferruccio was nine years old. 'We went to the Hotel Erzherzog Carl—the hotel for princes and celebrities—and were lucky enough to meet Rubinstein. My father managed to have me introduced and to "get me heard" ["*farmi sentire*"], as he was pleased to express it. I can still hear that terrifying "*Fagli sentire!*" ("Let him hear you!"). He never met anybody at a café or in the street without telling him all about "my son". And he would end by bringing the stranger back to the hotel, bursting in and dragging the new acquaintance along with him and shouting at me those dreadful words "*Fagli sentire!*" . . . If he accommodated my father with a small loan of money [he would be described as] "a thoroughly good man", for the state of the exchequer was then, and always was, the weak point of my father's administration.'

Between the close of *Doktor Faust* and Busoni's own end is a significant parallel; in the last years of his life he was increasingly interested in the work of younger musicians. As a matter of fact, he had always shown this curiosity. Felix White once bore witness to this in the following words: 'I recall how, one morning in Bechstein Hall, in 1902, Busoni gave an hour of his time listening, and afterwards giving much good advice and encouragement, to a callow but enthusiastic youth of eighteen, quite unknown to him or anyone else at that time, who came to him with a long piano sonata. May I add that this is no vague recollection or random hearsay, for the youth in question was myself.'

Another parallel to the Nietzschean end of *Doktor Faust* is the fact that the music was finished by another hand. To Philipp Jarnach, one of Busoni's disciples, this great task was entrusted. He carried it out in a self-effacing, yet authoritative manner. He knew his master's mind, and to it submitted his own.

I have referred to the deep impression made upon me by that first Dresden performance of *Doktor Faust*.[1] The conductor was

---

[1] The production of this work at the 1956 Berlin Festival was remarkable (I should guess, from photographs I have seen) for Helmuth Melchert's gargoyle of a Mephisto and for Fischer-Dieskau's foxy-looking Faust, which must have been in strange contrast with his sombre, pondering voice.

Fritz Busch. His attitude, I remember, was of almost palpable reverence, and under his direction the work was awe-inspiring. I am aware that this impression was partly due to the awestruck attitude of the audience, but chiefly it was the result of the performance and production as a whole. The stage designs were by Karl Dannemann, who produced an enchanting picture for the Gardens of Parma and an even more impressive scene for the cathedral interior. Robert Burg sang the title-role with measured power, though his tone was too restricted at the top of his register. The Mephisto was Theo Strack, a most intelligent actor and singer with the right kind of dramatic tenor quality for the part.[2] The finest singing, however, came from Meta Seinemeyer as the Countess. I believe I am right in saying that this fine artist sang that night under great difficulties. The story was that she had had a fall at one of the final rehearsals, and was in great pain during the performance.

After the final curtain and the silent tribute to the composer, as I have already remarked, I walked the streets of Dresden, for the moment overpowered. I remember doubtfully wondering whether we in England should ever truly understand such a work as *Doktor Faust*. To do that we should have to be in agreement with Busoni's theory of opera. In Busoni's opinion, the music of an opera must be an organic whole; not that the music is independent of words or stage action, but that its *wholeness as a musical form* is independent of these things.[3] The fact that *Doktor Faust*, like *Wozzeck*, consists of a succession of musical forms shows what Busoni was aiming at. He wanted the whole to be regarded as a musical form. The weakness of the argument is that it assumes that one musical form added to another must necessarily produce a third form. On the other hand, it is true to say that, since an opera can embody every style of music known to twentieth-century man, the present-day composer can use opera—as he can use no other medium—for his complete self-expression, can pour into it the full sum of his experience as musician-explorer.

[2] On this point of making Mephisto a tenor, Ernest Newman once wrote to me: 'His [Busoni's] is the poorest Mephisto in music—a screeching creature whom no one can take seriously.' My own impression was that Strack's Mephisto was all the more sinister for being a tenor.

[3] This view is also borne out in some of Britten's operas.

NINE

An English Violist

WHEN MY friend Lionel Tertis telephoned to say he was staying the night in Norwich, and would I call that evening to hear a viola of which he was very proud, I at once accepted. I went to his hotel, and he took me to his room and showed me two violas. 'I want you to tell me which of these is the older instrument,' he said. He extemporized on each in turn. Both had the mellow tone of an old instrument.

'Difficult to say,' I told him. He was delighted. Holding out one of the violas, he remarked: 'Sounds like an old instrument, doesn't it? But it's new. It's one of the Tertis models.' Then he played another cadenza with firm, strong bowing. In the small room the tone sounded like a dozen violas in unison.

This model viola was the result of much experimenting and a desire to reduce the weight of the instrument and to make it easy to handle. It was a token of a great player's gratitude for the joy afforded him by the instrument, to which, after early excursions with the piano and the violin, he had devoted all his powers. Over a hundred of these models have so far been made by Arthur Richardson of Crediton, and others have been made according to the same exact measurements and instructions in France, the United States, Australia, South America, and elsewhere.

All these instructions, with diagrams, are set down in Tertis's little book *Cinderella no more*, which is also a fragment of biography. There we learn that this eighty-year-old master violist, now living in semi-retirement in Devon, was born in West Hartlepool of naturalized British parents (Russian and Polish) and was brought up in the East End of London. He attributes his passion for music to his father, Alexander Tertis, a Jewish minister whose singing quality at the synagogue attracted many worshippers.

Several years later still, a certain young writer, spreading his wings in the *Daily Telegraph*, was impressed by that same quality in the playing of Alexander's son. That writer was one of 'Father' Robin Legge's junior critics and had been sent to the Albert Hall to hear Kreisler and Lionel Tertis play the *Sinfonia Concertante* of

Mozart. Beauty of tone, beauty of phrasing—these were the qualities which captivated the young critic in this performance. He was fully conscious that he might be overdoing it, that his writing might give him away as being a new boy. None the less, he let himself go in these words: 'For the performance of this work, our own Lionel Tertis had been invited to join him [Kreisler] and these two, each a master of his instrument, combined to create a spell of wondrous pure sound. The cadenzas (specially composed by Kreisler for this occasion) were given with such profusion of tone that, with eyes averted, it was hard not to believe that, in the double-stopping passages, one was hearing a string quartet.'

That junior critic is now writing these words and, looking over the storehouse of performances which his memory has since built, he still thinks of the playing of that Mozart concerto, little known in England until then, as one of the brightest of them all. In retrospect the two players seemed to be absolute equals, and yet there was a time when Lionel Tertis sat at Kreisler's feet. 'For me,' he writes, 'the experience of hearing him [Kreisler] was like falling in love'; and he singles out especially the glowing tone, the peculiarly personal phrasing, the manly grace of his bow-arm, above all, the *vibrato*.

There, I think, is the secret which, together with tone and phrasing, distinguishes Lionel Tertis's playing, his *vibrato*. That was the thing he concentrated on when Beecham invited him to help improve the tone of the strings of the London Phil-harmonic.

One of Lionel Tertis's admirers was the late Earl of Leicester. The natural sympathy existing between them was the outcome, I like to think, of their unceasing quest for an expressive beauty of tone, both in the art of string-playing and in the art of living. One evening, at Lord Leicester's request, Lionel Tertis played the *Chaconne* of Bach in the great entrance hall at Holkham in the dark. Such were the acoustics that Tertis, forgetting the mechanics of performance, found himself, passive and awe-struck, listening to his own playing.

When Lord Leicester died, it was the happiest of thoughts to invite Tertis to play in Holkham Church at the funeral. As one who played an insignificant part in that eloquently moving tribute, I felt how wonderfully fitting this gesture was—one spirit calling to another, both of great and singular gifts, and utterly possessed by music, both wearing with ease the beautiful garment of modesty. It was a unity of spirit, it seemed to me, comparable to that which filled the air on that golden day when Kreisler and Lionel Tertis together played Mozart.

TEN

A True Musician

THE OTHER day I went to my book-case to verify some date or other, and there fell out from between two books a leaflet which was printed on that occasion of the late Lord Leicester's funeral to which I have referred in the previous chapter. On the outside it read: *Thomas William Coke, 4th Earl of Leicester; born 9th July, 1880, died 21st August, 1949*. There were also some notes I had made as to the music which was played at the service in Holkham Church.

Before the service, I see that I played on the organ, at least on part of it (for there were a good many ciphers on some of the stops), the music of the Resurrection Angels from Elgar's *The Apostles* and an improvisation on a Tallis tune. Later in the service, I played, as best I could, the Angel's Farewell music from Elgar's *Gerontius*, which was much loved by Lord Leicester. On this same precarious organ, with great trepidation, I also accompanied Lionel Tertis, who, with power and wonderful tenderness, played the Serenade from Delius's *Hassan*, which somehow was not in the least incongruous, and Bach's *Come, Sweet Death*.

Recalling that sad but greatly uplifting occasion, I could not bring myself to realize that seven years had since slipped away. To those of us who enjoyed his friendship, Tom Leicester has never died, so vivid and endearing are the memories we have of him.

I first met him at the time I was bringing out my study of Elgar. It was at Turner's Studio, the Chelsea house of my friend, Mrs Valentine Fleming. I remember the pleasure I felt when he told me that he intended giving the two Elgar volumes to his daughter Mary for a Christmas present. Soon after, I met him again, with Lady Leicester, at Adila Fachiri's house in Netherton Grove, off the Fulham Road.

Almost imperceptibly our friendship grew, drawing its sustenance from music in general and Elgar's in particular. Although I knew he was an amateur violinist, it was not for many years that I heard him play, and that was something of a revelation.

I was then Rector of Warham, Norfolk (which was one of the livings in his gift), and I had suggested that it would be a delight to many if he gave a violin recital in aid of the fund I had opened for

the restoration of St Mary's, one of Warham's two churches. After
a time, he told me he had persuaded Lady Fermoy to join him in
giving this recital, which took place in the library at Holkham before an invited audience of parishioners and friends.

Before this concert took place he had asked me one morning to
rehearse some of the music with him. He played Bach—a slow
movement, I think, from one of the sonatas. It was a revealing experience. The tone, for one thing, was superfine, the phrasing, so
elegant, so informed with musicianship.

At the recital itself, his playing was quite lovely. Every phrase
spoke of devotion, of single-mindedness. What impressed me was
the absolute balance of each performance. No excessive expression
intruded and yet an unfailing warm-heartedness suffused it all.
Amateur the playing may have been, but here was an instance
where the word, rescued from the scorn heaped upon it by Lord
Rosebery's famous words, recovered for once its proper meaning.

The poise which marked Tom Leicester as a player was also
evident when he listened to music. He had a fine collection of
records and nothing gave him more pleasure than to play some of
them on the partly home-made gramophone which he had rigged
up with amplifiers in such a way that his friends could listen in the
library without hearing any of the attendant reproducing noises.

I have spent many happy times listening to those records.
Sometimes it was a Delius programme, sometimes Menuhin in a
concerto or the *Requiem* of Fauré. One evening we listened to the
whole recording of *Gerontius*. On these occasions, except for an
occasional quietly spoken exclamation, he rarely made any comment. Nor did I feel the need of expressing my enjoyment of the
records. These were moments to refrain even from good words.
In the music's after-silence, I would look through the windows to
the distant darkening trees and the fading western sky, and think
there was hardly a better way than this to enjoy music—no one
there expecting to be applauded.

Although he was a devotee of Elgar, his was not a one-composer
mind. For Delius he had an almost equal enthusiasm, and we
sometimes listened to records of French and Spanish music, of
certain of Vaughan Williams's works and of opera, for example,
Turandot and *Otello*. He was one of the comparatively few among
English music-lovers who had a taste for Bruckner. He used to
tell me how, as a young man, he tried to get Henry Wood to intro-

duce this composer's symphonies to a London audience. 'But who's going to pay for the parts, me boy?' was Henry Wood's objection, and Tom Leicester would half-mimic the pitched-up, penetrating voice.

I recall a particular performance of *Gerontius* at the Norfolk and Norwich Festival when, because of a personal sorrow, he was almost overwhelmed by the music. Even then he was outwardly composed. On another occasion when, at my suggestion, he invited Angus Morrison to give a recital at Holkham (again for the funds of Warham St Mary's), I noticed that, during one of the *Goyescas* of Granados, of which he was greatly fond, he slipped out into an adjoining room and there I later found him alone, listening through the half-opened door. It so happens that this particular piece of music communicates to me an intangible and quite indefinable emotion, especially when Angus Morrison plays it. I am always inclined to believe that such an emotion is uniquely one's own, that it cannot be precisely the same as that which is stirred by the same music in another listener, however sensitive. But in the case of this work ('The Lady and the Nightingale') I used to feel that Tom Leicester was affected by it in almost the same way as I was. There were passages in *Gerontius*—the dialogue of the Angel and the Soul, for example—where I felt the same was true. I have rarely felt a closer correspondence of musical emotion with any other friend.

In early days, he met with much opposition from his father in following his musical inclinations, and especially in studying the violin. He sometimes told me of those conflicts. Only through his utter devotion to music, and the encouragement of one or two understanding friends, did he prevail. His determination to master the violin was entirely right-minded. One had only to see him hold the instrument ready to begin a performance to know that he was a natural player. His many-sided duties at Holkham and in Norfolk required him to be practical and busily active, but sometimes while he was discussing the manifold affairs of the estate or planning the day's arrangements, in fancy I used to think of him as caged in a world of ceaseless cares and charges. Never for long could he deny the persistence of music in his thoughts, 'the dominant's persistence, till it must be answered to'.

ELEVEN

Remembered Voices

How HARD it is to make real again the memory of a voice! One can only play with a shadowy symbol of it. For that reason we must think well of the gramophone, although it can sometimes juggle curiously with the quality of a voice, whether singing or speaking. Looking back, I am surprised to find how few voices have impressed me sufficiently to tempt me occasionally to recall them, certainly, very few speaking voices. Henry Ainley's I think of as a royal and separate voice. Those who heard it only by radio missed its immense power. You had to be in the theatre to feel its moving richness and strength, and I shall always regret that I saw him so little in Shakespeare. Ainley as Macbeth is a fond memory. The purely intellectual spectator found there much to criticize, no doubt. Indeed it was not a study to satisfy any but those whose delight was in the music of words. It was as if the riddle of Macbeth's character had been regally cloaked in velvet.

I used to wonder what Ainley's thoughts were when he was broadcasting. Did he think of his audience as being in a vaster theatre than any he had played in before; or did he look upon broadcasting, with its studio audiences and pernickety young producers, as a smaller occupation than playing on the stage? Can the praising letters from a thousand listeners give the satisfaction that comes from the applause in a theatre? The oily smell of grease-paint, the knock on the dressing-room door, the faint orchestra, the quick hush as the auditorium lights go down, the pleasurable anxiety before the first entrance—can broadcasting offer a full compensation for the loss of all this? Henry Ainley in a broadcasting studio! I think of him there as a lion in circus captivity. And I thought of him so when, after I had recalled some memory of him in an article in the *Sunday Times*, he wrote me a grateful and wistful letter.

But I was musing upon human voices and, in doing so, had all the time at the back of my mind the voice of Chaliapin. That was a sound which became part of one's life, an elemental sound. Whether he sang from stage or platform he seemed to me to be a man capable of conveying the experiences, not merely of one race or one generation, but of the whole world since the beginning. An elemental sound! He would sing Beethoven's *In questa tomba oscura* and the image would be of a grim and ancient rock; or Grieg's *An Old Song* and it would be of a hill-sheltered lake; or Rimsky-Korsakov's *The Prophet* and it would be of a great roaring wind breathing a glorious elation. It mattered not to what age, or to what country or to what style the song belonged, this singer was able to enfold it, to make it his own, so that the song was enriched by his artistry. Some thought of him as being primarily an actor, but, in thinking so, they overlooked one thing, namely, that even when it became less tractable, his singing-voice was an essential factor in his peculiar dramatic power. It was like no other man's voice, and it was used like no other. Under his spell in the concert-hall or opera-house, I sometimes thought that to meet him would be like talking to some utterly unreal person. When I did meet him, I was surprised to find him no more abnormal than any other famous actor. This, I remember, was at the Savoy Hotel, London, on the occasion when, to mark some anniversary or other, the Gramophone Company made a presentation to Chaliapin. They had enquired what he would like best and he, to make sure, had asked for one of his recordings made in gold. It was a motley gathering, journalists, gramophone people, broadcasting people and the odds and ends of society who always find their way to these little ceremonies. Chaliapin was tired but affable. Soon after I met him, he surprised me by taking me aside. There, in a corner, he began telling me one fantastic story after another. Except that they always seemed about to become improper, and that one was about the singer, Lablache, I cannot now recall the tales in substance, only Chaliapin's superb acting of the various characters in the stories. I remember, too, being astonished, also embarrassed, that he should take so much trouble for an audience of one casual passer-by. Had he been on the Covent Garden stage he could not have delineated those figures with more detail or more *finesse* of inflexion; so that I began to think that in his imagination he was upon such a stage and acting before a crowded house.

Neither prose nor verse can communicate such a voice as this to those who did not hear it. Mere description cannot even catch its shadow; and to be telling of its effect upon the senses is like beating the air. That, of course, is true of a remembered landscape, of the earth's scent on a misty summer morning, of light in the sky.

G

It is true of all music, for what is 'stealing and giving odour' but a confession that the love-sick man could find no words to speak of music exactly and must fall back upon another and parallel sensation? It is true of a great part of human experience. But how uniquely true it is of the memory of a voice, that we cannot by the arts of writing encompass it.

There was once a time when every month or so I could hear John Coates sing in the Chelsea Town Hall, and on occasions I had the pleasure of hearing him sing one of my own songs. But how can I convey the healthy, exuberant effect of his singing? I can recall incidents, of course; how, for instance, on one occasion he sang Gerrard Williams's setting of *It was a Lordling's Daughter*, one he had often sung before, and seemed to be finding a new and slightly bitter aspect of the tale while he was singing; how, in a setting of *Shall I Compare Thee to a Summer's Day*, he would bring the song to full lyrical flower at the words 'when in eternal lines to time thou grow'st'. I can hear again with what delicacy he would spin the phrases of *Die Mainacht*. But, to one who never heard this singer, there is no way of conveying the youthful zest of his singing, the precise tuning of his merry and of his melancholy notes. One can only say that this was an English voice; that the style, too, was so truly English that, like the qualities of Purcell, Elgar, Vaughan Williams, and of the English character itself, it could not be precisely analysed. One can only—remember.

TWELVE

Schoenberg and the Homberg

WHEN MR ERWIN STEIN's *Orpheus in New Guises* was published, I was surprised to learn that it was, in fact, his first
book, for he has for many years been well known as a teacher and
especially as an expounder of Schoenberg. Many of us were
thankful at the time to receive these essays in a single volume, for
the author's intense sincerity and singleness of mind could the
better be appraised. The broom was widely applied to bring together these scattered leaves on Mahler, Britten, Webern, Berg
and, of course, Schoenberg. Consistency of mind binds and uni-
fies them.

Erwin Stein was a pupil and friend of Schoenberg, and we therefore turn inquiringly to the chapters on this composer, especially
to that dealing with the twelve-note system. Incidentally, it is
unfortunate that this system of composition is continually referred
to in these essays as 'twelve-note row', seeing that the English
word 'row' has two pronunciations. Perhaps in some future
edition, Mr Keller, who worked closely with the author in trans-
lating his articles, will consider using some other word for *Ton-
reihen* which will be less of a gift to the philistines. 'The most important difference between key and row' is, in print, not the
happiest sequence of words.

Not even in Vienna was Schoenberg received without question
in the early days. This, in Mr Stein's words, is what happened
when the String Quartet in F sharp minor was played there: 'A
well-known critic got to his feet and shouted, "Stop it". People
forgot their drawing-room manners; part of the audience joined
in the riot which others tried to silence.'

The incident takes me back to a performance of *Pierrot Lunaire*
(which at first had started similar storms in Central Europe) at a
BBC Concert in the Westminster Central Hall, London, on 7th
April 1930. Not that there was a riot this time. On the contrary,
the work was well received, partly because of the meticulous performance which Mr Erwin Stein had devotedly prepared with
the Pierrot Ensemble and, in the formidable role of the re-
citer, Erika Wagner (all fanatical specialists in this music), and
partly because the work had already been heard in London.

Indeed, on that earlier occasion it was given twice in one day.

Even those English critics who had hitherto set their faces against Schoenberg fell under the spell of this strange work, this astonishing last act of the heart-tormenting drama of Romanticism. For, now as then, it does astonish us to find a composer of Schoenberg's ingenuity and mental strength expending his resources on a theme so dated and decadent as Giraud's moonstruck Pierrot. Even when we take into account the date of his birth (1874, only twenty-one years after Brahms was beginning to be talked about), his Viennese environment, and the involutions of his complex personality, even when we bear in mind all the influences and forces which played upon him in early years, we can still marvel at the nature of Schoenberg's career. Like Einstein, he was that kind of phenomenon in whom mathematics extends into mysticism, in whom romantic and pedantic are not merely reconciled but become one and the same; so that, at one moment he would be searching for the utmost refinement of expression, of tone and dynamics, in order 'to exteriorize the subconscious', and at the same moment he would be able to over-simplify the whole process by declaring, 'I write what I feel in my heart', which, I suppose, is Schoenberg's way of saying: '*Le cœur a ses raisons que la raison ne connaît point.*'

Always he insisted that the twelve-tone scale did not fetter him as a composer. Nor did it liberate him. Following this scale, a composer could either be as cold as an engineer or 'as laymen imagine, may conceive in sweet dreams—in inspiration'. A composer's power of expression depended only on the degree of his creativeness. He could be just as original ('original or moving' are Schoenberg's words) with old or with modern methods.

In brief, the twelve-tone scale is not a formula. The system is not an end in itself, but a means, comparable in this sense to the old system of counterpoint. In the past, the uncreative composer, even though he was completely versed in counterpoint, could never have used his knowledge to produce a masterpiece. Nor can a master-work ever be expected from a present-day composer lacking the spark of originality, merely because he has mastered the twelve-tone scale system.

The average listener can grasp that point without any difficulty. Where the problem begins for him, in twelve-tone scale music, is in distinguishing between the work of an inspired and an un-inspired composer. Schoenberg acknowledged that whenever audiences had shouted his music down, it was because of the dissonances. This was foolish of them, he seems to imply, for 'dissonances are consonances which appear later in the overtones'. But this does not answer the question: how is the ordinary would-be follower of the new music to distinguish between the dissonances of the genius-composer (such as Schoenberg or Alban Berg) and those of the arid doctrinaire?

In Mr Stein's exposition of Schoenberg, this is one of several points which I would much like to discuss with him in conversation. Another is the point he makes about the 'three typical mirror-forms of the melodic motif: inversion, retrograde motion, and retrograde inversion'. Whereas these forms change 'the physiognomy of the motif', they do not change its structure. To illustrate the point, Mr Stein tells us that Schoenberg took a hat and turned it in all directions, saying: 'You see, this is a hat, whether I look at it from above, from below, from the front, from behind, from the left, from the right, it always remains a hat, even though it may look one thing from above and another from below.' In the same way, he explained, a theme inverted or played backwards will seem different from the basic form, and 'yet they are the self-same motif'. But is there a strict parallel here? In the apprehending of a musical theme, the time period is, *in itself, an integral part* of the experience, whereas this is not true of the envisaging of a hat.

But whether I am questioning or agreeing with his statement, I find Mr Stein, in everything he writes, singularly stimulating. Especially satisfying are the brief essays on Alban Berg, whom I met in Florence in 1933 and can never forget, so tragic and ill did he look.

It is certain that Opera can never continue to develop as if Berg's *Wozzeck* had never been. That it is an opera to be fully appreciated by the specialist rather than the average music-lover is revealed by the naïve association of the 'common' chord of C major with the prosaic idea of money and also by the calling in of musical forms to frame each incident in the drama. But the evocative power of the music is such that it has lured many an English listener even into so deep and dark a wood as the tragedy of poor Wozzeck.

Even more than that of his master, the music of Berg, though we may be aware of its structural principles, holds us chiefly by its emotional content, as, for instance, in the *Lyric Suite*, which grips attention by uncanny skill in the invention of sonorities, and, at one moment, deigns to give us a clue by quoting *Tristan*. Although he was a pupil of Schoenberg, it would be nearer the truth to regard the two as co-pioneers in the same perilous expedition, and the comparatively early death of Alban Berg even more than the death of Schoenberg was an immeasurable loss to the Viennese Orpheus in his striving after self-renewal. As Mr Stein truly says—and it does need to be said—the appeal of a work of art depends less on systems and methods than on personality. As in religion, so in the arts; wisdom and vision are begotten, not by theories, but by the spirit of individual genius.

This is the quality which has attracted Mr Stein to the music of Benjamin Britten, whose art he expounds with unique understanding. In an essay on Britten in relation to his English background, Mr Stein chides Orpheus Britannicus for neglecting to exploit more fully the richness and variety of the English language. Britten's remarkably imaginative use of recitative is surely a sign that at least one composer is intent on repairing this neglect.

THIRTEEN

Some Elgar Letters

AFTER receiving a request from G. Bell & Sons, the publishers, that I should undertake a biography of Elgar, I wrote to ask for the composer's approval.

MARL BANK
RAINBOW HILL
WORCESTER
11th May 1931

DEAR BASIL MAINE,

Many thanks for your very kind letter: if anyone is bold enough to publish such a work as that proposed I should be delighted to know that you were writing it; I can say no more than that. I never read anything about myself if it is possible to avoid doing so and do not know where I stand or rather, *sit* for I have had lumbago and broke a tendon or something of the sort.

I shall be glad to hear what happens to your efforts in the proposed or any other direction, and they will always have my good wishes.

With kind regards,
Believe me to be,
Yours sincerely,
EDWARD ELGAR.

MARL BANK
28th May 1931

DEAR MR BASIL MAINE,

Many thanks for your letter: the work suggested could not be in better hands but I seriously think you should hesitate before making any drastic change in your literary pursuits. I fear the interest in my music is too slight and evanescent to be worth such concentration as you propose to devote to it.

It is proposed that I shd contribute certain articles about myself to one of the popular papers. This I may do. Wd this handicap you in any way?

Probably such things if they ever come into being wd be forgotten by the time your book came to sight.

Kind regards,
Yours sincerely
EDWARD ELGAR.

The letters referred to in the following are those from Elgar to Jaeger, lent to me by Jaeger's widow.

MARL BANK

RAINBOW HILL

WORCESTER

19th November 1931

DEAR MR BASIL MAINE,

I am so sorry your letter has remained unanswered so long, but I have been away.

Before you begin to select anything for use from the letters, I shall be glad to see them; this I might do with you the next time I am in London. I always avoid writing letters when possible and I imagine anything existing might give some very misleading notions. I think I have some from other writers which might be interesting.

With kind regards,

Believe me to be,

Yours sincerely,

EDWARD ELGAR.

MARL BANK

RAINBOW HILL

WORCESTER

23rd December 1931

DEAR BASIL MAINE,

I suppose nothing will divert you from your fell purpose, so how would it be, if you can bear anything so dull, if you came here for (say) a weekend and we could talk. There would be food of sorts and probably drink and it wd give me great pleasure to see you: obvious drawbacks are (a) Dogs (b) myself (c) isolation. All good wishes for now and 1932.

Yours sincerely

EDWARD ELGAR.

MARL BANK

RAINBOW HILL

WORCESTER

24th February 1932

MY DEAR BASIL MAINE,

I have been having a bad time with influenza since New Year's day: I have managed to dodge it for several engagements but have not really retd to normal status.

If you can face this winter weather I shall be glad to see you: my surroundings are of the simply severe—or severely simple kind and I wd do what I can to make you welcome and *all* I can to prevent any ill effects from the exuberant attentions of my Dogs.

Yours very sincerely,
EDWARD ELGAR.

MARL BANK
RAINBOW HILL
WORCESTER
3rd March 1932

MY DEAR BASIL MAINE,

If you can face the rigours of this house I shall be delighted to welcome you—if you really do not mind dogs.

Let me know your train and day and I will meet you. You probably know that Paddington is the only way. *Shrub Hill* here is the station. I shall be delighted to see you: if you are 'cunning in your eating' and drinking (T.T. & Vegetarian etc.) all can be arranged.

Yours sincerely,
EDWARD ELGAR.

At this stage, Elgar was irked by the lengthening list of queries from author and publishers; and here is an early reference to what was to have been the Third Symphony.

MARL BANK
WORCESTER
13th October 1932

MY DEAR MAINE,

I am sorry that the work is being persisted in. I wish your publishers cd let me die in peace.

I fear there is nothing to say in regard to the new Symphony or anything else: things take shape without my knowing it—I am only the lead pencil and cannot foresee.

I shall be delighted to see you—give me some idea—say after Nov. 5th. I seem to remember that is an auspicious anniversary;—let us put your MS. & mine on a good Guido Fawkes bonfire and have done with it.

Kind regards,
Yours sincerely,
EDWARD ELGAR.

A letter from Sir Landon Ronald some time later, relating to the new symphony.

THE GUILDHALL SCHOOL OF MUSIC,
JOHN CARPENTER STREET,
VICTORIA EMBANKMENT, E.C.4.
June the sixth: 1933

DEAR BASIL MAINE

... For your extremely private ear, I would like you to know that I carried out all the negotiations between the BBC and Edward for the Third Symphony, and that I got him terms which I don't think any other composer had ever had, for writing a similar work.

Yours sincerely,
LANDON RONALD.

A reply to my suggestion that I should include in the biography some of Elgar's letters to Richter.

MARL BANK
RAINBOW HILL,
WORCESTER
2nd December 1932

MY DEAR MAINE

Herewith the letters: I do not see how or why anyone can be interested in them but as there is nothing objectionable—do as you think best.

The dogs were proud of your kindly recognition—the hedgehog and his (her?) brother are hibernating and unconscious, I will deliver your message when they fare forth in the spring.

Best regards,
Yours sincerely,
EDWARD ELGAR.

The publishers were wanting to bring out a limited edition (20 copies) of the two volumes bound as one, and in vellum, and signed by Elgar.

MARL BANK
WORCESTER
5th January 1933

MY DEAR MAINE

I am truly sorry your horrible project matures: God help us! Of course I will sign the copies if necessary and if it is of service to you.

I saw a paragraph saying that the book was written by you 'with the *collaboration* of E. E.' that is wrongly worded—the publishers may say with my '*approval*'—I shall not see the book and, rather, I shall not read it—I have read nothing about myself since 1900 and must keep to my rule;—there are sundry 'lives' or such things, extant but I have never seen them. I found out by accident in conversation that you have been holding forth (on the wireless) on my troubles in the concert days or nights: I was not aware of this at the time or I shd have referred to it when I saw you: you may have thought I was a fish-like cold blooded creature—but I really am not so.

I have no doubt that you have done wisely in your selections from the letters but I cannot conceive that people can be interested.

Best regards,
Yours sincerely,
EDWARD ELGAR.

A reference to the first International Congress of Music, held at Florence in May 1933. (During the Congress, Richard Strauss inquired after Elgar and asked me to bear him his greetings. Elgar was intensely pleased.)

MARL BANK
RAINBOW HILL
WORCESTER
14th April 1933

MY DEAR MAINE

I do not much like the idea of placing the autograph on the covers.

I hoped to have been at Florence but I gave it up; I wish I had known you were going.

Let me hear when you return.

Dogs well and send messages of affection.

Yours sincerely
EDWARD ELGAR.

The two volumes are now published, and the first letters come from Sir Landon Ronald and C. Lee Williams, and, after a week or two, from Elgar.

THE GUILDHALL SCHOOL OF MUSIC
JOHN CARPENTER STREET
VICTORIA EMBANKMENT, E.C.4

May the fifth 1933

MY DEAR BASIL MAINE,

I must just write you a line, because I am really excited about having received a copy of your biography of Elgar from the Publishers.

It was responsible for keeping me up till one o'clock this morning, and although I have only read a little more than half of it, I am simply delighted with it.

I want to be one of the very first to most heartily and sincerely congratulate you upon having done your work magnificently. It is a great achievement, and will undoubtedly be the standard biography of a very great man.

You know what extremely intimate friends he and I are, and I can honestly say that had the book been about myself, it would not have given me a quarter of the pleasure that this one has. . . .

. . . I thank you very truly for the pleasure you have given me, and hope you will accept my appreciation in the spirit it is meant.

Believe me,

Yours sincerely,

LANDON RONALD.

THE GUILDHALL SCHOOL OF MUSIC
May 9/33

MY DEAR BASIL MAINE,

What splendid notices your work has had! Bravo! I saw the great man on Sunday and made him sign my copy with a dedication, which he did very unwillingly! He swears he'll never read it! I don't believe it. But he spoke *so* nicely about you.

Kindest remembrances,

Yours v. sincerely,

LANDON RONALD.

MARL BANK
WORCESTER
18th May 1933

MY DEAR MAINE

The awful thing has happened and the publishers have sent two volumes; for all your wasted trouble I thank you: I never

have read anything about myself since 1900 and I do not propose
to begin now alas!

Yours sincerely,
EDWARD ELGAR.

The River Teme and the Second Symphony.

The last message I received from Elgar—he was too ill to write,
but managed to sign it. When I had visited him in the nursing
home during this final illness, he had been talking about a part of
the River Teme which he wanted to show me. 'When I am well
again, I shall take you there,' he said.

NURSING HOME
WORCESTER
Dec. 4th 1933

Dictated

MY DEAR MAINE,
　　　I knew you would do it! You literary men, as I warned
you, always make for Ludlow and that part of the country in
connection with the Teme. This shows the degradation that comes
from reading books. The Teme I want to show you is the lower
part which meanders among rocky woods and private farms for 25
miles and is practically unseen & unknown except to me in the 2nd
Symphony and several other people of goodly havings. You shall
be instructed some day.

Yours sincerely,
Signed—EDWARD ELGAR.

Two letters from Carice Blake, the one written just before her
father's death, the other after the Memorial Service in Worcester
Cathedral. (There is an obvious likeness between the handwriting
of father and daughter, though Elgar's sweeping hand needs more
space and frequently resorts to abbreviations.)

MARL BANK
WORCESTER
Feb: 16th, 1934

DEAR MR MAINE,
　　　I thought it best to open your letter to my father, as he is
so seriously ill now that he is not reading his letters—He had
another relapse last week, but has rallied from it and his physical
condition is quite fairly good again, but he is in a state of quite

frightful mental confusion—which is a most dreadful state of things to deal with. I think it may go on quite indefinitely, each attack leaving him on a lower plane of vitality. If any clear moment comes in which I can show your letter of course I will—I know he would be most interested in all you say—

Yours very sincerely,
CARICE S. BLAKE.

MARL BANK
RAINBOW HILL
WORCESTER
March 4th, 1934

DEAR MR MAINE,

I am so grateful for your understanding letter and also for your kind thought in sending the proof sheet of your article—which I thought was quite beautiful and embodied everything that should be said.

At present I can only feel so thankful that nightmare of illness is over for him—and, as I hope and believe, he never did find out what it was. As for being alone with his memory, it is as you rightly say the thing I wanted but have been entirely unable to achieve until today. I wonder if you were at the Cathedral on Friday. It was so perfectly arranged. He was so very definite in his wishes that there should be no memorial service in the usually accepted sense of the words, but this did not come in that category at all, and was a tribute I am sure he would have loved.

The future seems an utter blank—we were such tremendous friends.

Yours very sincerely,
CARICE S. BLAKE.

A letter from Carice Elgar Blake about the fragments of the Third Symphony.

WOODEND
BROADHEATH
NR. WORCESTER
April 2nd 1939

DEAR MR MAINE,

I want to tell you that I have at last got your book—'The Best of Me'—I do not know why but it eluded me for months. I love all you say about him—and your feelings about the 3rd Symphony I do so understand. But of course the manuscript had to be given over to the BBC and it does seem to me a great safeguard for the future that the themes have been published. Perhaps I look too far ahead—but I had awful visions of people getting hold of it in about A.D. 2000! when there would be nobody left who would have known him, and trying to finish it.

Yours very sincerely,

CARICE ELGAR BLAKE.

From BERNARD SHAW.

AYOT SAINT LAWRENCE,

19th September, 1949

DEAR MR MAINE,

All I have to say about Elgar that I have not said already I inscribed in the copy of the *Severn Suite* he dedicated to me and sent to me. It was sold with all my other books at Sotheby's in July; and as the purchaser bought it on the understanding that no copy of the inscription existed I may not give it over again even if I had time.

But it does not matter, as you know as much about him as I do, if not more. I could tell you nothing printable that you do not already know. The critics are getting tired of his music. There is a very marked reaction in *The Times*, partly the fault of conductors who have not heard his works conducted by himself at the 3 Choirs Festival in Worcester Cathedral.

G. BERNARD SHAW.

FOURTEEN

Recessional: Thirty Years

I

WHEN I BEGAN to write as a music critic for the *Daily Telegraph*, one of my first major assignments was to travel to Prague for the 1925 Festival of the International Society of Contemporary Music. This was the second of this Society's festivals, held under the benign Presidency of Edward J. Dent. The Festival had been planned a year in advance at the Society's conference at Salzburg. 'My first major assignment', I say, although perhaps I ought to record as the very first, a recital by Heifetz in the Albert Hall, my notice of which, although it was set up in type, failed to appear. When I made inquiries, I was told that my judgement of Heifetz's playing was clean contrary to that of a senior staff critic which had been published in the *Daily Telegraph* a few days before. I still have a proof of that notice—the notice which was never published—and, looking at it again, I can still feel the first regretful pang of realizing that Heifetz would never have the benefit of reading those carefully praising words and of knowing the impression he had made upon a young critic, fresh and uninhibited in his enthusiasm. Still, I must say that the great violinist's career seems to have been unimpaired by the omission.

That Festival at Prague was a landmark in my early experiences of music as a critic, as it was also in the acknowledgement of English music abroad. Although there was only one important English work in the programme, and although even this failed to win the approval of the German critics, and although the performance of the work by the Czech Philharmonic Orchestra lacked intimacy, yet this first performance out of Britain of Vaughan Williams's *Pastoral Symphony* marked the first breaking-down of the indifference to English music which had existed in Europe since the end of the first World War, and the event will always be linked in my mind with the name of Adrian Boult, who, by his understanding of the work and by endless patience with the Czech orchestral players, managed wonderfully to transport the tenuous, fragile music to its new environment with a minimum of damage. Indeed, this performance and that of Bartok's *Suite des Dances* (composed in 1923 to celebrate the reunion of Buda and Pest) proved to be the peaks of that Festival. Talich, the Czech conductor, directed the latter. At that time, except for two violin sonatas, which Jelly d'Aranyi had played in London, I had heard few professional performances of Bartok's music. The *Suite des Dances* at Prague was immediately compelling, the more so since I had met Bartok several times during the Festival and had felt something of the elemental power which was contained in that small, spare frame and was always flashing from those piercing eyes. In some degree that power is let loose at the end of the *Suite des Dances*, a scintillating score unified by means of a *ritournelle*. Purposeful—that was the feeling conveyed by each of the movements. Already, through the precise rhythms, the bold orchestral colours, the drive, we knew that this was the music of an exceptionally strong, not to say tough, mind.

So, already in 1925, we had some idea of who were going to prove outstanding figures in European music during the next thirty years. Certainly, Bartok and Vaughan Williams would have to be reckoned with. Yet, sitting with Vaughan Williams and his wife [1] in a box in the Smetana Hall of the Obecni Dum for this notable performance of his *Pastoral Symphony*, I received the clear impression of a true humility in him. As a composer, he had, of course, long arrived. But the final verdict of 'greatness' was yet to come. Knowing his character as we do now, we cannot pretend to be surprised that he put on no airs on this festival occasion. However hard he tried, this endearing musician could never do that, could never put on airs. He had come to Prague, as the rest of us had come (Lady Ravensdale, Rosa Newmarch, Gerald Cooper and Hubert Foss were some of the English visitors) to hear all the music and see all the plays we could possibly manage and to learn something of the musical standards of this ancient capital. Of course we all went to *The Bartered Bride*. It was given one Sunday afternoon. Vaughan Williams, Adrian Boult, Hubert Foss and I went in a party and saw what V. W. later described to me as 'the worst *Bartered Bride* I've ever seen'.

Among the other composers represented in this early expedition into contemporary music was Malipiero with a dry, delicately fashioned work called *Variazioni senza tema*, and Krenek (then

---

[1] An arthritic cripple, Mrs Vaughan Williams had bravely travelled to Prague to hear this first European performance.

H

aged twenty-five and previously a pupil of Schreker) whose
2nd Concerto Grosso, gave me a perverse pleasure, as though I had
boarded a wrong train and, well knowing its destination, was
content to see what would happen on the way.

There were also works by composers less well known at that
time, Roland Manuel, Martinu, Georges Kosa, a pupil of Bartok,
and Paul Amadeus Pisk (whose *Partita* I followed from an im-
maculately penned manuscript score), a pupil of Schoenberg.

At intervals we had opportunity of hearing examples of contemporary Czech music. One was a nobly conceived cantata by
Vycpalek—is he now entirely forgotten in Central Europe?—
another was Janáček's opera, *The Cunning Vixen*. When I met
him then (on a pleasure steamer) Janáček was already advanced in
years, but in spirit a mischievous, practical-joking boy. At the
Aldeburgh Festival of 1954, I remarked on my impression of
Janáček to Erwin Stein, who, after listening to the Wind Octet,
included in a centenary concert of Janáček's music, said to me:
'Your description of him is exactly confirmed by this work.' In
his music, Janáček never grew old. Indeed, when we bear in mind
the period in which he lived (1854–1928), his rustic origin, and
the intensely, almost narrowly, nationalistic bent of his mind, we
can only marvel at the ardent, forward-looking spirit which is pro-
claimed in his music, whether the male-voice choral examples or
the extremely individual ideas and scoring of his orchestral works.
Like Bartok and Kodaly in Hungary, Janáček was an absorbed
student of the folk-songs and speech-rhythms of his country, and
much of his music stems from this knowledge, especially in its
fervour, its brusque humour and abrupt rhythms. In the first
quarter of the twentieth century, European music had hardly a
more strongly independent composer to show than Janáček. He
was a character, an original.

II

My purpose in recalling that occasion in Prague is to fix, as far as
possible, a starting-point for a brief comment upon the continuing life of music from that day to this; and the first thing to
note, I think, is this: in spite of the disruption and dislocation of the
second World War, it is extraordinary how continuous this life has
been. One of the reasons for this was the great exodus of musicians,
performers as well as composers, which took place in 1939 and a

little earlier and later, from Europe to the safe retreat of America. In this respect, the New World can be seen as a distinctly beneficent influence on the development of the music of the Old World. At the same time, as President Eisenhower observed in his address to the World Council of Churches, no country's motives are ever entirely selfless, and if European music was much blessed in the harbouring of Schoenberg, Krenek, Milhaud, Britten, Hindemith, and other composers during the war years (not to mention the scholars of music, such as Karl Geiringer) so also were American composers, as well as the country's musical life in general, immensely stimulated by the presence of these outstanding artists, some of whom were equally influential as teachers.

America, then, must be credited as being a factor in the continuous development of European composers during the conflict and prolonged anxiety of the period we are considering. The fact remains that the creative spirit of those composers could never have survived the uprooting and transplanting, but for the sturdiness of the force working through them. In England alone the upsurge of the spirit and will to compose which took place in the years between the two wars was phenomenal. We had known nothing like it since the short, swift summer when we took over the madrigal from the Italian masters and, grafting it on to the rhythmic vigour of the English language, brought it to a full and singular flowering—not for three hundred years, that is to say.

Soon after the Prague Festival, the International Society for Contemporary Music held another at Zurich, and it was on this occasion that William Walton, already known abroad for his *String Quartet*, was represented by his *Portsmouth Point*. Thereafter, English music was flowing at high tide with work after work from Bliss, Bax, Ireland, Frank Bridge, Holst, Vaughan Williams, to name only those who come immediately to mind. Yet we were as diffident as ever in forwarding our claims to be considered seriously as a force in contemporary music. The calumny of 'the land without music' we were content to leave unanswered. Occasionally there appeared in our daily and weekly Press a plea 'for fair play for English music' such as Henry Peacham had made for Byrd and Dryden had made for Purcell. But, as usual, we English lacked showmanship, that quality we affect to regard with horror. Must the showman always be a vulgar fellow? Showmanship, in the best sense, implies that a man should take care to reveal the best of himself at the most opportune time. So with a nation. The English rarely take that care.

Or, if we do, we go to extremes. At present, in our eagerness to make the most of the genius of Benjamin Britten—a genius which has so stunned the English that we are only just showing signs of recovering—we are in danger not only of overshadowing other native composers of his and a younger generation,[2] but also of over-looking the pioneering role played by those inter-war composers whom I have just mentioned.

Some of this forward movement, which was already in existence during the first World War, derived its impetus from Elgar, not so much from his music as from his achievement, which was in fact to bring English music again into the main European tide; and some of it was impelled by an admiration for the musical mind of Vaughan Williams. To illustrate these points, two incidents come to mind.

When I was living in Chelsea, I had a telephone call early one evening from William Walton, who lived near. He said he had just completed a concerto for viola and would like to come round and play some of it from the manuscript.

He arrived soon after, and, in the indescribable idiom of his pianoforte-playing, gave me some idea of the orchestral score, and occasionally a sketchy *vocalise* of the viola part. I clearly remember thinking that there were passages in this *Viola Concerto* which were reminiscent, by implication rather than by statement, of the Elgarian voice. The influence *is* there, without a doubt, even if it does not always show itself so brassily as in the *Crown Imperial* March.

The other incident was an evening spent with Arthur Bliss at his Hampstead home. There was to be a broadcast of the *Tallis Fantasia* of Vaughan Williams and we were to listen. Not many minutes after the broadcast was ended, the telephone rang. 'Sure to be Robert Nichols,' Arthur said. 'He always rings after the *Tallis Fantasia*.' Then followed a long communication in the next room, largely consisting at this end of 'superb', 'magnificent', 'that wonderful episode where . . .'—the most breathlessly *exalté* telephone talk I have ever overheard.

[2] To name a few, Rawsthorne, Tippett, Fricker, Malcolm Arnold, Wordsworth, Oldham, Hopkins, and (as medicinal as his cartoonist namesake) Searle.

In criticism of whatsoever art, there are those who are ceaselessly hunting for influences; others shy at the very mention of the word. To speak of the influence of one composer upon another is not necessarily to relate them as tyrant and slave. Admittedly not obvious, nevertheless the influence of Vaughan Williams was, though temporary, as real as that of Stravinsky upon the growth of Bliss's musical mind; or as real as Ravel's was for a period upon Vaughan Williams himself, or as real as that of Sibelius upon a composer so dissimilar as Bax, or as Prokofiev's was upon Ireland. (In my possession is a letter which John Ireland wrote to me at the time he was delighting in his discovery of Prokofiev's *Third Pianoforte Concerto*; and others written when he was under the spell of the symphonies of Sibelius.) Such influences, in a forceful composer, enhance rather than dilute originality. They do not show themselves in features of imitation or coincidence. Rather can they be said at a given period to enter the blood-stream, producing a new condition in the composer's activity, so that he could not thereafter convincingly write in any of his earlier manners, even if he so desired.

If this is true, as I believe, of individual English composers, it is equally and similarly true of our native music as a whole. Since the early years of this century the terrain of English music has been invaded by powerful forces of influence. The arrival of the fabulous Diaghilev Ballet in London marked the beginning of several infiltrations, of which Operation Stravinsky was most far-reaching. The election of an Englishman, Edward Dent, to the Presidency of the International Society for Contemporary Music, brought our younger composers into touch with the new tributaries of musical thought and creation which were in full flow soon after the end of the first World War, and we became aware not only of the strong influence which was being exerted upon ardent disciples by Schoenberg, but also of the claims of such single-minded composers as Malipiero and Hindemith, as well as of such independent spirits as Berg, Milhaud, Pizzetti, and the volcanic Bartok.

But, although the English Muse came into contact with these and other influences, and although, in some instances, they considerably transformed her manners and behaviour, her essential character remained unchanged. During one of the early performances of Walton's *Viola Concerto*, given at the Three Choirs' Festival,

Elgar was seen pacing up and down behind the orchestra gallery
and deploring that such music should be thought fit for a stringed
instrument. The concerto was too new for him to realize that in
some of its inflexions, Elgarian influence, though not obvious, is
strong. In the 1920's we heard much of Stravinsky's influence
upon Bliss, but at a choral concert in Halifax in 1954, when the
music of Bliss (*Morning Heroes*) and Elgar (*Sea Pictures* and *The
Music Makers*) formed the programme, one of the younger English
critics [3] was impressed by the musical relationship between the
two composers. Delius and Vaughan Williams have also force-
fully impressed themselves upon younger writers, the former upon
Peter Warlock and Moeran in particular, the latter upon George
Dyson and, less obviously, Herbert Howells and Patrick Hadley.
Yet, in the music of Howells and Hadley especially, and also in
that of Gerald Finzi, such influence has promoted rather than
stifled originality; while, even in an apparently insulated composer like Edmund Rubbra, the sensitive listener may yet feel the
ancestral currents running.

The point is worth making, for in the welter of ideas and sensa-
tions which was let loose in the inter-war period, the English
Muse might well have lost her individuality as completely as did
the English Miss, who, for the sake of spurious advancement, retired behind the Hollywood mask; whereas, in the music of Britten,
to take a single example, her individuality has been so far pro-
nounced as to emphasize regional origins and so far insistent as to
choose a local and very minor poet for her temporary partner.

III

Surveying the general scene of English music at the present time
and comparing it with that of thirty years ago, we receive an impression of sturdiness and immense fertility. It is as though we are
looking down from the air upon a landscape of rich variety through
which run two or three main roads, and also a number of by-
roads and cross-roads which tend to confuse the eye in its attempt
to judge a general direction. No arterial yet appears. Such change
as is apparent is comparable to the incidental physical changes in
the countryside itself due to varying vogues in farming and the
over-spilling of towns. Fundamentals remain.

[3] Ernest Bradbury of the *Yorkshire Post*.

From earliest times, one of the fundamentals of English music has been its clinging devotion to the English language. In Vaughan Williams, Bliss, Ireland, Moeran, Howells, Hadley, Britten, Tippett, and others, the native choral tradition wells up again with reassuring force. But at the beginning of this thirty-year period we passed through some disquieting experiences, where the composer, having tried a number of side-paths without seeming to get anywhere, tentatively took the way of dissonant counterpoint, letting the vocal lines collide and clash in the hope that, if not divine fire, perhaps at least a few flying sparks would come of it. Having passed unharmed through the fiery furnace of *Sacre du Printemps*, *Les Noces*, and *L'Histoire du Soldat*, and having indeed assimilated every horrific tone-cluster let loose by these and other progressive works, the English composer was emboldened to introduce these wolfish sounds into the fold of English choral music—hitherto carefully protected, except for one or two raids such as the *Demon Chorus* in *Gerontius*—so that, ultimately, even so conservative a flock as the Royal Choral Society had no alternative but to capitulate. When this Society first sang Walton's *Belshazzar's Feast*, there doubtless were many of its old supporters who were as shocked as though their moral sense had been affronted. But it was not so very long before the Royal choralists were singing, and its audience were listening to, the contrapuntal forthrightness of *By the Waters of Babylon*, without trepidation, if not exactly with affection. Just below the surface of their consciousness was the same thought, I dare say, which prompted the enlightened Dr Burney to write two centuries ago: 'I am convinced that provided the ear be at length made amends, there are few dissonances too strong for it.'

The instance of the Royal Choral Society I have quoted with intention; for this is a body typifying the average English choral singer, who, during the period we are considering, has so multiplied in number that no village Women's Institute can now feel wholly accomplished until it has formed a choir. Some present-day English composers, Vaughan Williams and Britten among them, occasionally write with these lowly choirs in mind, and as long as they intermittently write works of this kind, we can be sure that English music is moving in the right direction. The reader may think that this sounds like one more argument in favour of bringing all art down to the level of the average (which in practice always means the lower-than-average) intelligence. If so, the reader is mistaken. I have never subscribed to that dreary fabrication, the apotheosis of the common man, not even when I was one of the BBC's regular preachers of the Gospel of Appreciation. On the other hand, experience teaches that it is as gross an error to make a cult of the remotely uncommon as of the common. The true artist, of course, is never ordinary in his art, however ordinary his daily life may seem to be. Neither is he so un-ordinary as to be wholly cerebral. And in nothing does the true composer-artist reveal his artistry so unmistakably as in his idea of what is apt music for voices.

In the winter of 1954 it so happened that in a single evening there were heard in London two works with contradictory ideas of the nature of vocal music, namely, Schoenberg's Opus 27, being four pieces for mixed choir, and a motet *Blessed be the God*, by the English composer Racine Fricker. Whereas in the latter the composer has the sensibility to modify his formidable instrumental style to accommodate his singers, it would be difficult to imagine what music in general, not to mention the human vocal apparatus, will be like in the era, if ever it arrives, when writing like that of Schoenberg's Opus 27 will be accepted as constitutionally apt for singing.

Though by no means the only country with a choral tradition, England has never neglected that tradition for long at a time. Sometimes the guiding influence has been the Church, sometimes the concert hall, sometimes the social or industrial unit, sometimes the opera house. Towards the end of the period upon which I am reflecting, was a year (1954) which may well be singled out by historians as the *annus mirabilis* of English opera. During that brief period were produced Lennox Berkeley's *A Dinner Engagement* and later his *Nelson* (a charmingly evocative work which by any other name but *Nelson* would perhaps have been received more favourably), Britten's *Turn of the Screw* and Walton's *Troilus and Cressida*, and, in addition, there was news of the completion of Michael Tippett's *The Midsummer Marriage*.[4] Whether some of these, together with Britten's previous operas and such works as Bliss's *The Olympians*, will hold their places in the repertory ten or fifteen years hence, or be put under glass as exhibits of a plant which flowered too marvellously and too late, we cannot yet judge.

[4] Produced at Covent Garden, 27th January 1955.

We can, however, already be certain of one beneficial influence that this audacious border in the pleasure-grounds of our native music will have upon the general scene. Apart from the choruses and *ensembles*, the necessity to write effectively for the solo voice which is incumbent upon every opera-writer, has brought these English composers into the closest practical touch with both voice and 'verse', and this cannot but augur well for the future of English choral writing. What can be sung, if not exactly with ease, at least without producing a sore throat, by a solo voice, can, with obvious modification, be sung as a part in a piece of choral writing. Entire preoccupation with instruments has rarely resulted in an entire composer. The voice is as essential to the control of musical thought as breathing is to the control of the voice.

IV

On more than one occasion I have written that the future of English music depends upon faithfulness to the choral tradition, and there is good evidence that several contemporary English composers, older and younger, are fully aware of this. Not only have they been continually stimulated by works from the G.O.M. of English music, in styles ranging from the *Benedicite* to *Five Tudor Portraits* and from *Sancta Civitas* to the homely *Seasons* written for Women's Institute choirs, but they have been prompted also by some notable writing, both in original works and in translation, by contemporary English poets, a number of whom have taken full advantage of the singularity of the English language as to variety of rhythm and of what by analogy we are accustomed to call colour.

We must bear in mind, however, that in the development of music or of any art, there is no one line of progress. Also there is the possibility that our judgement as to what is progressive in contemporary music may be reversed when the musical creations and activities of our time pass into history; and even the verdict of history is by no means unalterable, as we know from the constant changes of vogue, even within the fifty years of the present century, as to the Italian painters of the Renaissance, to quote only a single instance. When we also acknowledge that the term Modern Music is as imprecise in meaning as the term Renaissance Art, we shall very properly shrink from anything so bold as a generalization regarding the honeycomb of present-day English music.

Therefore, if in this argument about English music the reader thinks there is too much stress upon the need for cultivating the choral or the lyrical tradition, he is not to conclude that gifted symphonic writers or composers whose *forte* is chamber music have been overlooked. In any case, the fertility of some of these needs no special encouragement. If I have drawn attention to the field of English music for voices, it is not in any generalizing frame of mind, nor because I have mistaken that one field, however wide and accommodating its dimensions, for the entire landscape. Nor have I done so because I believe music for voices to be the highest or purest form of music, although I am bound to say that I cannot see why the perfect fusion of words and music, the organic whole which is the ideal of the collaboration of composer and poet, and of librettist and opera-writer, cannot be as essentially pure as symphonic music. The very fact that the human voice is capable of producing words and musical sounds simultaneously is surely an indication, to say the least, that the union of music and voice is an eminently natural art, and surely we need no proof that marriage, even if it is imperfect, can be just as pure as bachelor- or spinster-hood.

More than one living English composer has shown himself aware of this need for cultivating the field of vocal music, notably Britten and Tippett. Of Britten's music it can be said that the greater part of its inspiration has been derived from the word, whether verse or prose. No English composer of our time can equal Britten in giving the impression that he has hit upon an exact musical counterpart to the verbal phrase *au premier coup*. If art critics are permitted to use the word 'painterly', as they seem to be, we may perhaps speak of Britten, in this context, as the most 'composerly' of composers. His professionalism is as complete and sure as that of the French impressionist painters.

Tippett's association with the choir of Morley College has been a vital element in the development of his technique. By nature an aloof and sometimes private composer, he has been compelled by this working association with a body of singers, to keep in touch; so that, even though there are considerable asperities in, for example, his contribution to the *Garland for the Queen* (the setting of Christopher Fry's *Dance, clarion air*), they are neither wilful nor insoluble, and, in a good performance, they undoubtedly give to singers, as well as to audience, that sense of purpose and high achievement which distinguish the same composer's *2nd String Quartet.*

If Alan Rawsthorne seems to some people to be rather less accessible than Tippett, I suggest that this may be due to his almost continuous preoccupation with instrumental thinking. If we think of his *Concerto for Strings,* to take a random example of his music, we realize almost at the beginning of a performance that we must be prepared for a nearly unrelieved intensity of experience, that, while we are appreciating the powerful counterpoints, we must pay the price of an uncompromising harshness of texture; that, while we are admiring the skilful deployment of parts by which an astounding bigness of tone is obtained in one episode of the sombre slow movement, we are compelled to acknowledge that this is done by making each line intent upon its course, with little regard for the others; that, while we can appraise the immense drive, as of a north-easter, of this concerto, we are all too conscious of its being a reproduction in other terms, of the exacting gale-force of present-day life.[5] In fact, we begin listening to such a work in a braced-up if rather grim mood of acceptance, well knowing there will be a religious avoidance of the beautiful sonorities inherent in string writing, well knowing there can now be no return to the sounds Elgar discovered half a century ago in his *Introduction and Allegro,* not even to those of Bliss's *Music for Strings.*

But a prolonged and unbroken north-easter soon takes toll, and this is as true of the spiritual climate of life as of the physical; and perhaps Rawsthorne would be wise, in his development as an artist, to permit occasionally the tempering influence of the voice to play upon his style. Not necessarily to make it less uncompromising, but rather to bring it that much nearer to human experience, as is the case with Tippett's development.

Even Tippett, however, like many another composer of our time, is uneasy at the thought of becoming too approachable. He has stated his conviction that, if he is to write sincerely, the understanding of his music is bound to be confined to the *coterie.* This 'I am not of your element' attitude is precisely what the true artist

---

[5] Since these words were written, the *2nd Violin Concerto* has been produced (24th Oct. 1956) and here Rawsthorne's rugged style is more compact and conciliatory, and the meditative under-current more compelling.

seeks to avoid, or rather instinct guides his steps away from such a disastrous pitfall. The very word *coterie*, redolent of membership, blackballing, taboo, and private emblems, is antithetic to the purpose of art. True, the artist had better not be a preacher, but, in the nature of the case, he must be a communicator, and the smaller the number of the excommunicated, the better for his health of mind and wholeness of spirit. This is not to deny to art the inclusion of symbolism; only the symbolism must be capable of being sooner or later universally understood. Music, after all, is wholly composed of symbols. What has happened during the period of time which I am now considering is that, through the media of mechanized music, greater and greater numbers of people have come to understand the language and behaviour of those symbols. So conditioned have they become that they are now capable of breathing the same air as those giants educationally known as the great composers. No one expects the creative composers of the present and near-future to re-write in their own ways the music of the past. Of course not. On the other hand, they should ever be conscious of the fact that their music, if it is to be accounted part of a living historic process, must always convey the feeling that it *needs* the listener for its complete fulfilment. For that reason alone, the composer must always be wary of a too precious privacy, and to guard against his sometimes understandable inclination to rarefy the air around him.

In this matter, the responsible critic can play a part of considerable usefulness, especially if he is of the younger generation. Fortunately, we have in England a number of young music critics who are more than promising. Indeed, they appear to have bypassed the promising stage and suddenly, between 1948 and 1950, to have appeared upon the scene as ready-made writers. That these young Daniels are able to pronounce judgement with an authority beyond their years is due, first, to persistent preparation and study during the war-years, and second, to the remarkable activity of critical scholarship which was going on in England (as well as elsewhere) between 1919 and 1939, and of which they have been able to take full advantage.

In many respects, the work of these young men and women is praiseworthy, notably for good sense, for acute observation, for the quick detection of anything less than genuine, and for a fresh-minded approach, whether in appraisal or exegesis, of contemporary music. What appears to me to be rather less than admirable is their frequent unanimity of opinion. It is not a good thing for any English composer, whether elder or intermediate or on-coming, to be almost certain of a chorus of approval or, equally, of disapproval, for any new work he produces. A case in point is Walton's *Troilus and Cressida*. There were so many music-followers in England who, having heard of this opera being on the way, were wanting it to be a success, both for the composer's sake and for the sake of English opera, that critical judgement, in some instances, was in abeyance at its first performance. I cannot pre-tend to have read every one of the published judgements, but of those I did read, not one indicated the real reason for the lack of true climax in this opera, the reason being that the device of climax (like the device of repeating some of the verbal phrases of the dialogue) is too often employed. As with Matilda in the Cautionary Tale, the composer of *Troilus* grows too fond of shouting 'Fire!' It is all very well to write of the sextet as a towering climactic moment, but I find this is not true to actual experience of the music, as distinct from a pre-reading of the score. I am open to correction, but no one among the younger writers, as far as I am aware, made this point. No one wrote that Walton's *Troilus*, full of good things though it is, and often effectively theatrical, is well-nigh the most calculated of operas.[6]

This tendency towards unanimity, this over-indulgent attitude to English music of our own time, is the one reservation I make in an otherwise admiring approval of the younger critics now en-gaged in journalism. I hope seniority is not too heavily underlined when I express the hope that they will discover how much greater a service they can devote to contemporary music, not least to that of English composers, by an objective candour than by a brilliant-surfaced one-mindedness which has servility at its core. Through such objectivity and independence they could be especially in-fluential in continually warning the present-day English composer against the fatal heresy that music which is accessible to a few initiates is the only worth-while pursuit, and contrariwise, that music which invites the approach and understanding of a full-

---

[6] Never for a minute are we in doubt as to what emotion, in this or that episode, we *ought* to be experiencing, but librettist and composer, for all their close consorting, rarely succeed in bringing it home as an actuality.

house audience, is on that account meretricious. Many a composer
has been lured into oblivion by that heresy. It is part of the critic's
function to save the composer from himself. The task of the critic
of music is more taxing than that of critics of other arts. In music,
it is far more difficult to detect nonsense. On the other hand, the
music critic must be alert in every faculty to make that detection,
for once a composer's nonsense is accepted, he is safe for at least a
lifetime, and, as we have often known to our cost during this
present century, a good and honest composer can sometimes write
musical nonsense and be convinced he is still composing music.

Explaining her new writing in a pseudo-philosophical apology,
Gertrude Stein perpetrated this: 'Anybody can get tired of anything and so they do not know it but they get tired of feeling they
are understanding and so they take pleasure in having something
that they feel they are not understanding.'

Embedded in that rigmarole is a valuable grain of truth; and
when our contemporary composing systems are entered into the
historical text-books, when all our New Musics have grown old,
we shall perhaps recover that truth—one we should never have
forsaken—namely, that, though in one sense Music must eternally
remain the Sphinx's riddle, no living and abiding communication
can ever come from the precious tone-juggling and acoustical pro-
positions which are offered in the name of composition by groups
of merely pedantic theoreticians.

Looking back to that Prague Festival of 1925, which was my first
prolonged experience of the zone of climate which music was
about to enter, I am surprised to find how comparatively little the
actual constitution of the art has since changed. The music I
heard then, of Bartok, Vaughan Williams, Janáček, Krenek, Martinu, Malipiero, and others, was not essentially different from that
which is heard in England today, whether in concert-hall, opera-
house, or by radio. Schoenberg's 'new world of sound' had already
spread its wings over the European music of thirty years ago, and
while some found its influence chilling, others welcomed a new
'security'. The same is true today. To a number of central
European composers, Schoenberg is a prophet who has given them
a fresh vision of musical form, with an endless vista of fascinating
possibilities. To others, and most English composers are among
them, his 'new world' is too remote and exactingly lonely, and we

must look to such composers to restore to twentieth-century music something of that humanism which, with rare exceptions, has always been characteristic of the arts in England, for, while it is true to say that the genuine artist must be unworldly, we may learn from the careers of a number of our native contemporary composers, from Vaughan Williams to Britten, that the artist can yet be 'in touch' without sacrificing one degree of that unworldliness. Even in the demoniac cauldron of present-day activity, the genuine work of art will rely for its eventual appeal, not upon out-of-the-way subject-matter or startling treatment, but upon the maintenance of a current of sympathy between the maker of the work and its recipient, that is to say, upon the establishment of a fellow-feeling. What kind of musical personality is the composer? That is always the vitally interesting question.

From a Diary of English Festivals

Aldeburgh, 20th June 1955

WE HAVE had a day of English music; first, a morning concert at the Jubilee Hall, then Britten's *The Turn of the Screw* in the same hall this evening. Though this display of our native genius has been given with no particular theme in mind, it has been an absorbing experience. The morning session brought us music which we rarely come upon in routine concert attendance—Frank Bridge's *3rd String Quartet*, for instance, three of Purcell's once-neglected *String Fantasias*, and a Housman song-sequence called *Along the Field*, for voice and violin, which Vaughan Williams wrote years ago and has since rescued from a drawer. Then there was a *Sonatina* for solo flute (needing all the expertness of John Francis to put it over) by a very young composer, Richard Bennett. Decidedly, this last essay suffered from no lack of ideas.

Fecundity is also the first quality that strikes one in hearing again Frank Bridge's strenuous but finely written Quartet. Always the composer's natural exuberance is apparent in the intensity of expression—not least in some of the writing for 'cello—but in this, and in other of his chamber works, he comes to grips with his multitudinous invention, and, even while ceaselessly exploring, imposes that discipline upon his writing which, after the lovely muted slow movement, enables him to bring about the culmination of a splendidly vital finale.

We can be grateful to Benjamin Britten for including this act of homage to his former teacher, no less than to the Zorian Quartet for the warmth of their performance, so contrasted with their restraint in those ever-astonishing fantasies of Purcell. (In the now-famous five-part *Fantasia* on one note, by the way, they were joined by Britten as second viola, monastically devoting himself to the one note, as though he had come to the point of renouncing all the heady wine of composing for the pure spring-water of that single tone.)

After Purcell's beautifully managed cross-currents of sound, Vaughan Williams's duo for voice and violin, except when he falls

<hr/>

[1] Radio scripts are marked *

back upon the folk-song manner, had an austere, not to say parched sound. Well as this sequence was sung and played, its studied meanderings were memorably unalluring. Perhaps that is because we are getting so mortally tired of Housman's graveyard mind.

The first thing to say about Basil Coleman's production of *The Turn of the Screw* is that it has been most cunningly adapted to the restricted resources of the Jubilee Hall, where the stage is so small that one is always fearful lest a character in walking off should make a final exit into the sea. Wonders are performed in the continuity of the scenes of which this opera consists—so much so, that with a minimum of distraction, and indeed with many advantages, especially a cast notable for good acting (not least from the boy, David Hemmings), Britten's music gets its own way, and by means of many brilliant touches, often comes within sight of the ideals of music drama.

Of Mrs Piper's libretto, it is enough to say that it has proved malleable to the composer who uses it to create a continuous atmosphere of tension around the governess and the two children. His self-set problem of writing for a cast of six high voices is astoundingly turned to account in a texture of closely-woven themes, enhanced by the varied colouring to be obtained from a chamber orchestra of some fifteen instruments.

The orchestral prologue and the interludes before each scene are, in fact, theme and variations, and although there is clearly an element of artifice about this scheme, the effect is to bind together the bundle of scenes by the music's sheer power of evocation.

But in opera, admiration is not enough. The composer must also make us care for his characters; and when the characters are born of a brain like Henry James's, it is imperative that the composer, to make them credible and appealing on the singing stage, should breathe into them what life he can.

As a point, consider the scene by the lake, where the contest for Flora's soul is fiendishly difficult to make convincing, the more so since it is entangled with the feat of writing an *ensemble* for four high female voices. Also, Mrs Piper's libretto strikes one as highly intelligent to the point of near-absurdity in Act II, Scene I, where the two ghosts start an argument and even come to blows—unless we are to understand it as a little bout of shadow boxing.

For a true Jacobite, it may be retorted, such things are not at all

I

hard to accept; indeed, I suppose, for them music is unnecessary for blood-chilling purposes. But for the others—and in the opera-house these will be a numerous majority—the swift strokes of Britten's music will do much to make acceptable this two-minded story, this excursion into mystification, because they will recall that the theme of Parsifal-like innocence versus guiltiness is one common to several of the composer's stage works.

A musician noted for his preciosity of speech was heard on one occasion addressing an orchestra during rehearsal: 'Gentlemen, in this episode I want everyone to be shadowy together.' That is what the audience at *The Turn of the Screw* must endeavour to be.

Aldeburgh, 23rd June 1955
'A structureless flux of novelty'—the phrase is W. H. Auden's, and he uses it to describe each new experience of the human spirit. To me, *The Turn of the Screw* was not exactly that when I saw it the other night, because I had been able, through broad-casting, to make earlier acquaintance with the music. Moreover the composer has taken guard against a first impression of struc-turelessness—and the reader, I trust, will not hold me responsible for the length of that word—by imposing a formalism upon the opera, namely, air and variations doing duty as *entr'actes* in a way similar to the use of the same scheme in his third Canticle.

So, seeing the opera a second time this evening, I was at liberty to observe the actual performance in more detail. Almost the first tribute, I think, must go to the E.O.G. Orchestra, from Olive Zorian, leader, through all the talents, to percussion-master James Blades. Playing under the composer's precision beat, they have given a most lucid account of the exacting score.

As to the singing, I have already remarked on the difficulty of getting the words over in so many high-voiced roles. The most successful in this matter have been Joan Cross as Mrs Grose, Peter Pears and Alexander Young alternating in the part of Quint and each with his own interestingly distinct portrayal, and Olive Dyer and David Hemmings as the children.

The temptation to watch and listen to the performance of this young boy, David Hemmings, as a feat is great, but of course must be resisted. Fortunately the producer, realizing this, has toned down any tendency to show off, except in the piano scene. Here young Hemmings is altogether too good at pretending to be playing the clever parody music. The episode is a distraction. We are watching an act 'put on'. Illusion vanishes.

Another point: would not the blood run colder if Arda Mandikian's Miss Jessel, so admirably icy in appearance, were less torrid, more horrid (or seeming so) in voice? As for Jennifer Vyvyan, I thought both as actress and singer she sustained the enormously difficult role of the racked Governess with uncommon distinction.

King's Lynn, 26th July 1955

When I last sat with the organist in the loft at Westminster Abbey, one November afternoon during the last war—it was a Civic Service—the organ kept up such a terrific pressure of sound, almost throughout, that I seemed to be deaf for many days after. (The player, I hasten to add, was not the Abbey organist.)

Now the fashion in organ-playing has changed. How much so we were able to judge from the excellent recital given on the Snetzler organ in St Margaret's Church here, yesterday afternoon by the present Abbey organist, Sir William McKie.

Except for the Bach *Passacaglia and Fugue* as centre-piece, and a *Fantasia and Fugue* by Parry for finale, everything was small-voiced, pure-toned and, in scale, nearer to a musical box than an organ in its more bloated sense. A pendulum-swing, of course, and a welcome one, to check that fanaticism which had almost succeeded in putting the organ in the altar's place.

Except for the Bach and a group by Sweelinck, Sir William's recital, which was fairly well attended, consisted entirely of English music. Specially interesting was the *Voluntary* of John Stanley, contemporary with the earlier part of St Margaret's organ, and beautifully suited in its liveliness to Snetzler's light tones.

The Mendelssohnian *Larghetto* of S. S. Wesley was delightfully 'scored' by the recitalist, as was the inevitable *Rhosymedre Prelude* of Vaughan Williams. But, at the close of the playing, my mind returned to the opening pieces of Sweelinck in order to remark two things, namely, the registration in the first of the *Chorale Variations*, cool and transparent as a mountain stream, and the overtones in the second of the *Variations* which were so prominent as to make the effect of bi-tonality, which, surely, was never for one moment in the composer's mind.

In the evening, over to the Guildhall of St George for a recital

of music for four-handed piano, the players being Ruth Fermoy
and Gerald Moore, alternating at treble and bass. In the audience
were H.M. Queen Elizabeth the Queen Mother, and H.R.H.
Princess Margaret.

The concert began with a Mozart sonata (K 497), the fine, free
invention of which was realized by these two artists with a remarkably unified sensibility, especially in the ebullience of the
finale and the sustained flight of poetry which is the *andante*;
at the end of the recital were two rarely-heard compositions,
Debussy's *Six Épigraphes antiques*, music fortunately salvaged
by the composer from his note-books and well worth hearing for
its fascinating exploration of sonorities, and as a perfect foil, the
attractive exhibition piece called *Allegro Brillant* by Mendelssohn.

Between these groups we heard more note-book music, a very
welcome performance of Brahms' *Liebeslieder Waltzes*, which were
given by the two recitalists, together with Margaret Field-Hyde,
Helen Watts, Rene Soames and Gordon Clinton, as the exceptionally well-balanced singing quartet, and so emphasizing how wrong
it is to suppose that this music can equally well be given without
the voices.

In writing it, Brahms freed himself from the heavy-heartedness
of the *Requiem* and thereby revealed to the world that he was deter-
mined to save himself from being a neurotic, which, because of his
strange inner struggle, was a possibility, by becoming an artist.

This was an enchanting performance by singers and players.
From the latter especially, an extra versatility—a gift as it were for
musical dialect—is required, if they are to capture the refinements
of the Brahmsian waltz manner, and one may gratefully say that
this stylistic feeling was continuously evident in the playing of
Ruth Fermoy and Gerald Moore.

Could one have wished for a little relaxation of facial expression
on the part of the singers? Possibly. But I shall not press the
point, for, in my opinion, this was one of the outstanding experiences
in the five-year history of this Festival.

King's Lynn, 30th July 1955

This evening I saw Emlyn Williams in his current production of
Dylan Thomas Growing Up. The production itself consists almost
entirely of lighting, the only props being a screen, on which the
poet's name is scrawled, and a chair. One would have thought the

more of this extravaganza, had one not been first of all spoilt by
the Dickens recitals, especially as some of the assumed voices are
the same in each entertainment. Albeit, this comic build-up of the
tragic young poet is rich in the overtones of suggestiveness.

It does not seem so long ago—actually it was before the war—
that Edith Sitwell wrote to thank me for calling attention to this
poet, then almost unknown, in an article in the *Sunday Times*.
Since then, as with Kathleen Ferrier, death has given him dominion.

There is now a D.T. vogue, and if this sounds like chronic
alcoholism, it is not altogether inappropriate; for during nearly
three hours of spell-binding, Emlyn Williams is surest of his laughs
when, as in *The Outing*, tippling is either the theme or the implication. The sot crying after the flying moon, the bottle growing
from the finger, the flag of Siam fluttering above a strange locale—
such wild irregularities are the stock-in-trade of the red-nosed
comedian. But in Emlyn Williams's hands they are lifted to the
plane of tragi-comedy. Such is his power and his magic, that even
while we laugh, we are inwardly weeping at the thought that this
poet's life should have been so brief an outing.

Norfolk and Norwich Triennial, 13th October 1955

A week or so ago the booking for this concert was hanging fire,
probably because of the inclusion of a contemporary symphony
in the programme. Possibly since then, would-be supporters began to realize that Sir John Barbirolli is hardly the man to be an
apostle of frightfulness, certainly not of quackery. Whatever the
reason, there was a good number of late tickets sold for the performance tonight of Stanley Bate's *3rd Symphony*.

The work is dedicated to Barbirolli, and in his directing of a
finely finished performance we had one more shining instance of
how he in turn is dedicated to every phrase of music his orchestra
plays. That is his signal quality and theirs.

One can understand his sponsoring of this particular symphony,
for it is expertly built and fluently inventive—the last movement
notably so—as well as lucid in exposition; and it is gratifying that
Bate has found so doughty a champion as Sir John, for being
neither a reactionary nor a cerebral system-composer, he would
otherwise be easily overlooked as things are in the present set-up
of the musical world. He is, for example, hardly likely to figure in
the Darmstadt Festival lists; and although this work with the rest

of the concert was broadcast on that wave-length, one would not condemn him by calling him a typical Third Programme composer. Present-day music so individual, so sane, above all so compelling in its dry manner of following up a wealth of ideas, is hard to come by; and when we reached the heart of the matter in the slow episode near the end, we knew we had made a new friend among symphonies.

This work had for prelude the *Cola Brugnon* overture of Kabalevsky and a lovely account of the Intermezzo from Delius's *Fennimore and Gerda*. The first is stimulatingly imaginative, and good enough music to be enjoyed without dragging in any of the usual nonsense about the party line. On the evidence of this racy theatre-piece with its touches of Rimsky-an brilliance, we may surely assume that Kabalevsky is no cabalistic composer.

On these occasions we always look to become more intimately acquainted with solo players of renown and the workings of their minds. We like to know if this former 'race apart' is preserving its integrity in the midst of the inimical forces of our time. Last evening, for example, for all Campoli's mastery, I had the uneasy feeling that as regards speed he was being lured by supersonic ambitions. No such thought could be entertained for a moment about Clifford Curzon, who was so wholly satisfying an interpreter tonight in the *B flat Concerto* of Brahms. This was an essentially big performance in which Curzon, Barbirolli, and the Hallé were equal partners, as indeed they must be in a work so closely concerted—to use the word in the pre-romantic sense. The bigness did not merely consist of technical mastery, consummate though this must be (and was) in pianoforte writing as exacting as we have here, but also and chiefly in the blending of rhapsody and immense control.

Except that every great artist is himself and no one else, I am tempted to think of Clifford Curzon as the Gieseking of our native pianists, and even that great player has not quite the same vein of poetry that Curzon has.

Nostalgia for the Ballet *

Whenever we indulge in the melancholy pleasure of looking through old programmes, we are almost sure to come upon one which touches an extra-sensitive spring, releasing a host of memories.

I was looking at such a one not long ago. It was printed on pink paper and carried on the faded cover this impressive piece of information: *Royal Opera House, Covent Garden. The World's Premier Theatre.* Inside was this odd programme: Part One: A film with the one word *Love* for title. Part Two: Lopokova and Massine in a series of new divertissements, and among them an item called *Ragtime* to music by Stravinsky. My memory of that evening is centred on that *Ragtime* diversion. Lopokova had invited me to watch from the side of the stage. At the end, the applause was so enthusiastic that I ignored the frantic signals a scene-shifter on the opposite side was making, though I saw him well enough. Part of the general excitement, I thought. As it happened, he was trying to tell me that the massive curtain was just being let down and that I was in the way; but before I could realize this, the curtain had swept me on to the stage, and there I was, mixed up with the dancers, who were taking their calls and their flowers. For a wild moment I did think that I might go back to my corner in a series of leaps, as dancers do when leaving the stage, hoping the audience would mistake me for Idzikowski, or some other member of the company in plain clothes. Fortunately, I did not act upon that impulse.

From that occasion at Covent Garden my mind travelled to another at the Alhambra, some few years earlier. That was the first time I ever saw the Diaghilev Ballet. Memory here is confused by the overwhelming richness of the experience. I know I sat in the Upper Circle. I know I was alone. I had seen Ballet before, of course, but this was an altogether strange joy. Of the master-hands that had brought about the potent magic of *Scheherazade*, knew almost nothing. At the end of the ballet for a few moments I was lost, and then, suddenly, became aware that the whole audience was equally spell-bound. Many rose to their feet and, like possessed people, cheered and cheered. Next me was a young woman who turned to me to say: 'This is enchantment.' 'It *is* enchantment,' I said. That was all. We did not speak to each other again.

That same night I also saw Massine in *Carnaval.* A few years later I met and knew him, as far as it was possible to know that enigmatic spirit. I was then a music critic for the *Daily Telegraph.* Robin Legge, my chief—Father Robin, as we called him— had decided that Russian Ballet should be one of my particular provinces. I was not slow to enter that land of so much promise. Massine said he would be glad to have me attend rehearsals if I wished, and whenever the company was in London I eagerly availed myself of the invitation. During one rehearsal I saw Massine at work inventing a new ballet, while a transcriber was recording the steps in a fascinating shorthand. At the end of another rehearsal I met Lydia Lopokova. I had been reading a book during the pauses and hold-ups, and she came over to ask me the title. I told her it was a novel by Hugh Walpole, and for some reason this made her laugh. In studied and almost too literal English she asked me more questions, and at each of my replies she laughed enchantingly. So began a laughing friendship, which will always be one of memory's delights.

At the name of Lydia Lopokova, more memories come crowding in. I hardly know which to choose. Allow me a momentary diversion to tell you of the little play in which Lopokova was to be seen in her first speaking part in English. This was several years later. It was a play by Merimée, given one hot July night in a house in Mayfair before an audience of friends. Two of the male characters were to wear big false noses which had been bought at Gamages, and I remember that, before the play began, the two actors were lying on beds while I helped to stick on these noses with gum. Owing to the heat, it was difficult to do this and I had to give about five minutes hard pressure to each. Now one of the actors had a mannerism: he would rest his left hand on his chest, palm upwards, then to stress a word, would, with that same hand, suddenly describe a semi-circle, ending with the arm rigidly stretched out. During the performance, at the climax of one of his speeches, his emphasis was such that the false nose dropped from his face. It fell neatly into his left hand and, with the semi-circular gesture, was flung into the audience. The next words were to be Lydia Lopokova's first in English upon any stage. They were not spoken. She was hiding her face in her hands and, laughing and crying, called out: 'I cannot, I cannot.' She did not see, lying like a crushed wild rose at her feet, the second false nose which had just then dropped from the other actor's face.

I take up again that faded pink programme and look at some of the names printed there. Besides Lopokova and Massine, there are Sokolova, Ninette de Valois, Astafieva, Ursula Moreton, Woizikovski, Slavinski and others.

Some of those names now are like illuminated pages in the

history of ballet. Even the sound of them carries enchantment, and each is associated with some memorable interpretation or other, a performance which derived a great part of its inspiration from the influence of one man—Diaghilev.

Diaghilev *

On 21st June 1911, at Covent Garden, Serge Diaghilev made his *début* in London. The programme that night was *Le Pavillon d'Armide*, *Carnaval*, and *Prince Igor*. Five nights later there was a Coronation Gala at Covent Garden at which one act of *Le Pavillon d'Armide* was given.

How shall we assess the achievement of this extraordinary man? One way is to imagine what the development of Ballet would have been without such formative influences as *La Boutique Fantasque*, *Petrouchka*, *The Fire-bird*, *Les Sylphides*, *Tricorne*, and other works—not that Diaghilev was an active partner in the creation of these ballets. His genius was rather in the choosing and teaming of the several artists for their creation.

Consider, for instance, *Tricorne*, one of the outstanding achievements of multiple authorship. The bringing together of Picasso for the *décor*, Massine for the making of the ballet, and Falla for the music was one of Diaghilev's most brilliant strokes. And with those names I shall always associate Woizikovski and Sokolova for their brilliant dancing as the Miller and his wife.

When I first heard Falla's music for this ballet, the outstanding impression was of its vitality and variety of rhythm. Later, the peculiar freshness of the harmony began to steal over the senses, and after that I began to appreciate the significance of those wry little tunes. Still later I began to perceive the essential quality of this music, namely its brilliant clarity. Recall the Miller's Dance, and you will realize that every phrase, every tone, every accent is given an edge such as we see when a dark cloud begins to efface the sun.

Massine, I think, never produced anything finer than *Tricorne*, which is as much as to say that Diaghilev never produced anything finer. For Massine was his choice for the devising of this ballet. As a union of the talents it is unsurpassed, although some think it is equalled by *La Boutique Fantasque*, for the making of which Diaghilev chose Derain for the *décor*, the music of Rossini delightfully arranged by Respighi, and Massine again for the creating

of the dances. Here again we think of Diaghilev as the chief in-
stigator of the work—a wonderful mingling of movement, music,
colour, dreams, wit, and childhood sentiment.

Diaghilev was always open to new ideas for his ballets, always
on the look-out. Perhaps you remember the spoon-players who
used to entertain the theatre-queues by producing the most
astonishing rhythms with a couple of spoons struck on the palm
of the hand and up and down the body? One day Diaghilev was
watching one of these experts and was fascinated not only by the
playing, but also by the easy graceful movements of the player.
Not long after, that same player, to his great surprise I feel sure,
found himself playing the spoons on the stage as a member of
Diaghilev's company in the ballet called *Les Matelots*.

Diaghilev was always like that, always searching for some new
manifestation of talent or of genius. We owe to him the discovery
of many a young musician, many a young painter, many a young
dancer. His name would deserve honour if only for one of those
discoveries. This, in brief, is the story: about two years after that
London *début* which I mentioned, Diaghilev was wanting a very
young male dancer for the part of Joseph in Strauss's *Legend of
Joseph*. The part was written for Nijinsky, but at that time he was
in South America. Diaghilev went back to Russia and started his
search. At last, in the Imperial Theatre at Moscow, he saw a
seventeen-year-old boy who had been studying drama and ballet.
Diaghilev knew immediately that he had found his Joseph. He
engaged the boy, put him under the supervision of one of the great
dancing-teachers, and let him dance in the *corps de ballet*. In a few
months the boy was dancing the principal parts. Then Diaghilev
did a bold thing: he presented this young dancer, first in Paris and
then in London, in the important part of Joseph. 'His dancing is
poetry' was the judgement of Paris, and 'a revelation' was London's
verdict. The boy's name was Leonide Massine.

In his early performances as the negro lover in *Scheherazade*,
Massine danced with such a fine frenzy that people began to forget
that they had seen Nijinsky in the same role. All this time and
then again in the years just after the first World War, Massine's
dancing had an extraordinary effect on the London public. I
often met him and attended many of his rehearsals. In the *Daily
Telegraph* I wrote several articles about him, in one of which I discussed some of his ideas about the future development of ballet,

ideas which eventually led him to reach that peak of dance-invention, *Choreartium*. Diaghilev fully appreciated Massine's uniqueness. 'The boy is remarkable,' he once said; 'why, he understands a thing before you have explained it to him!' But I often wonder what Diaghilev, with his prejudice against German music, would have thought of *Choreartium*. What would he have thought of a ballet based on Brahms's Fourth Symphony?

Poison gas! That was Diaghilev's description of the music of Brahms and of Wagner. He had his peculiarities. Even greater than his dislike of a long stretch of Brahms was his dismay at facing a long stretch of ocean. He was terrified of being on the sea. When he had to cross the English Channel, he would go down to the port of embarkation and hang about for days until the sea was quiet and looked like staying quiet. As for crossing the Atlantic, it was only after long agonies of apprehension that he ever consented to submit to that ordeal. He crossed over to America during the first World War. That was ordeal enough for the normal person. For Diaghilev it was an hourly death. During the voyage he used to pace the decks with Massine, as depressed and terrified as a man could be. Meanwhile various members of the company were ordered to pray in turn for him in the cabin. Not that Diaghilev was religious in any serious sense; but he was superstitious. There was not a moment during this crossing when he was not fearing the worst, and the worst became still worse as the days dragged on. Then at last, one foggy day, something did happen. The ship's sirens were sounding alarmingly. Diaghilev struggled into his lifebelt and rushed to the boats. He stood there petrified. And then someone said: 'New York at last, thank goodness!'

'New York?'

Yes, they had arrived.

Standing there in the fog with his lifebelt on, Diaghilev was too terror-stricken to move.

Let me briefly recall a number of other incidents: Diaghilev's discovery of an English dancer called Hilda Munnings, whom he re-named Sokolova after the famous Russian *ballerina*; the bringing into the company of an Irish dancer, who was at first given the absurd name of Patrikiev but was later known as Anton Dolin; many instances of Diaghilev slipping quietly into the back of the theatre, and the company, somehow sensing his presence, suddenly

keyed up and dancing at its finest; a London reception given to
Diaghilev and his artists—these social events were always a little
difficult to get going because the dancers were so shy, but this particular reception was enlivened by an amusing speech from
Diaghilev upbraiding the English for their conservatism. 'I bring
you something new,' he said, 'and at once you accuse me of bluff
[the last word with a French pronunciation]. Everything I do is
bluff! Always bluff!' Many other such incidents come to mind
serving as *entr'actes* to link the memories of the great creations
that this thoroughbred theatreman, by his unique faculty of
judgement, brought about—*Petrouchka, Fire-bird, L'Après-midi,
Cimarosiana* (that lovely thing), *Good Humoured Ladies, Carnaval,*
and, most brilliant of all, *Tricorne.*

Let's make a Concert

As with the building of anything worth while, there is a kind of
science, inexact though it may be, in the building of a concert programme. I have known some people who also made it an art. My
friend, Gerald Cooper, was such a man. In him, a practical sense,
good taste and wide knowledge were so well balanced that his
London concerts were models, both as regards the programmes he
presented and the artists he engaged for them.

Every concert, of course, is governed by its own circumstances.
A concert given by the Royal Philharmonic Society will naturally
be an entirely different problem from one given by a local philharmonic society. Every penny must be weighed in considering
the framing of a programme in a locality where the public is not
only numerically limited, but is also cautious in widening its experience of music—and this applies equally to the unfamiliar in
old and in new music.

On the other hand, even a local audience is not static. A constant stream of younger folk is always finding its way into the
concert hall, and it is always a good thing for any programme committee to include in their number at least one delegate from the
oncoming generation, or at any rate one who is in touch and in
sympathy with their ideas and preferences. Then the local society
is more likely to be resilient, and an equilibrium between contemporary and older musical works is more likely to be kept in view.

Are there any general principles to guide those who choose concert programmes? Indeed, there are. But I want here to single

out one for special emphasis. I do not propose to call attention to such obvious things as (1) the importance of choosing the opening item—for the average provincial audience it should not be too long (certainly the audience must not be plunged straight away into a symphony), it must not be too problematic and it must not be lugubrious; (2) the importance of contrasting, either in style or mood or orchestration, adjacent works; and (3) the great importance, in a miscellaneous programme, of deciding which work is to be the peak of the concert, so that it can be advantageously placed and so that performers may move towards it with a purpose. This will help to counteract the listlessness which is liable to descend at any moment during a concert given by an orchestra which is largely amateur. (It will often be found that a programme is most satisfactory when its trajectory of interest can be represented by a graph of which the highest point is nearer to the end of the concert than the beginning.)

These are elementary points. The principle I particularly want to stress here is that which I will label, 'One hurdle at a time'. Let us assume that a local society, bearing in mind its younger supporters, decides to include in one of the programmes a choral work by an English composer of the present generation. Suppose this work provided half of the concert and that the other half is to be built round a well-known instrumental soloist. One of the committee remembers that it is some time since they engaged a solo 'cellist. The committee agrees and a 'cellist is booked. At first sight the decision appears reasonable enough. Appeal to the younger, adventurous public in one part of the programme; in the other, make a more general appeal—that is the idea. But an important point has been overlooked. The inclusion of a contemporary choral work is a problem in the sense that it will call for more than an average amount of rehearsal time and still be an open question as to the extent of its drawing power. The choice of a solo 'cellist also involves a problem; first, his public is smaller than that of the solo violinist or pianist, and second, his repertory is extremely limited. Someone on the committee says, 'Must we have the Haydn concerto again? Can't we give one of the few other 'cello concertos?' 'We can't afford the extra instruments,' insists another member of the committee. And, of course, he is right.

Where, then, is the mistake? It lies in the ignoring (or overlooking) of the principle I have called, 'One hurdle at a time'. This imaginary concert is attempting to take two hurdles; first, the chanciness of a work new to the public; second, the doubtful appeal (Casals not being available) of a 'cellist playing in a hackneyed work. And the solution? No doubt about it: you must postpone your idea of a solo 'cellist until another concert when you can make him the central attraction and can spare a little from the kitty-bag so that he can be heard in one of the less overplayed concertos. If you must have a soloist for this present concert, why not engage a good but not too expensive violinist to play a concerto of Mozart or Bach, requiring only a normal orchestra?

There is no formula for making a concert. Of course not. But there are certain broad principles which, in my experience, are all too often forgotten, such as those I have briefly mentioned. Another is: choose the music first, the soloist afterwards—to choose a work to show off a particular player is an abomination. And how frequently do we meet with societies who forget the simple fact that the financial success of a concert is not in every case best promoted by cutting down expenses?

Recently I was looking at an 1837 programme of 'A pianoforte evening', with its jumble of piano works, songs, duets—and glees for light relief. To be sure, we do better nowadays. But that is not to say we cannot do better still.

Mancroft Echoes *

No one living in Norwich fifty years ago could ignore the church of St Peter Mancroft, its superb mass flanking the south side of the big open market-place. Wherever you lived in the city, you were almost bound to see it once a week or so as you moved about your business; or, sooner or later, when the wind came your way, you would hear the tumult of those rich-toned bells. All through my boyhood the clamour of those bells was an inescapable part of life's pattern. Their unique quality and resonance so filled my ears that for many years I was unable to think of any bells I happened to hear as being anything like as beautiful. Even now I have come upon only two or three examples which I have thought worthy to be included in the same company.

I don't know exactly how old I was when my father decided that I should be given organ lessons by the organist of St Peter Mancroft, Mr Maddern Williams. I remember it was just before the church was provided with a new organ, because my first few lessons were given on an old three-manual affair. The action of this old organ was so heavy that my young fingers could hardly cope with the keyboards even when they were uncoupled; when they were coupled, there seemed only one solution—

> *The abbé Liszt*
> *Hit the piano with his fist.*
> *That was the way*
> *He used to play.*

When I was sure the church was empty, I occasionally tried the same short cut; but the noise was so appalling that I used to frighten myself, especially if it was a winter's evening and the organ lights were enveloped by the deep darkness all around. But soon the new organ was installed and there was the excitement not only of pressing down ivory tabs instead of pulling out stops— that was then a new and fascinating experience—but also of trying, again when no one was about, the three ear-splitting reeds, called Tromba, Trumpet, and Clarion. There was also, on the lowest manual, a Tuba Mirabilis, but since I was already enamoured of the sound of another Tuba, the noble-voiced one on the Norwich Cathedral organ, this one, I am afraid, failed to win my affection. Raucous and hollow I thought it, and, when practising, I did my best to resist its vulgar allurement.

Once, however, I permitted myself to experiment with its possibilities in one of the pieces for pedal piano by Schumann, but in this I was discouraged by an unexpected interruption. In those days, the verger of St Peter Mancroft was a well-known local figure called Douro Potter. He was then aged about fifty-five, I should say. Tall, very upright, handsome, and of leisurely move- ment, he used to walk about the church with an air of complete ownership. This air was emphasized by a moustache, which was halfway in size between military and what you would call handle- bar. He had that high-coloured complexion which, with good reason, I always associate with trombonists. As a displayer of St Peter Mancroft and its treasures, he had every right to be described as creative; that is to say, he scorned parrot-talk and the deadly style of the parish church guide-book. He would first study his visitors and then adjust himself, as far as possible, to their level.

I always tried to fit in my organ practising during the lunch-

hour or some other time when I thought it unlikely that the verger
would be conducting visitors round the church. The occasion
when I was trying out the Tuba in the Schumann piece was, I
remember, well after one o'clock mid-day, and I was reasonably
sure I was alone. The coarse-voiced Tuba bellowed clumsily,
once, twice; the awful reverberation died down and I was preparing for the next entry. But before my fingers could come down
on the keys—'Just a minute, *just* a minute', someone was calling. I
looked round and there, to the left just behind me, was the face of
Douro Potter, his high-coloured complexion heightened into
purple. For a moment, we just stared at each other in silence.
Then, in an awed whisper, 'I'm very sorry,' I said, for by then
I noticed at the other end of the nave a group of six or seven
people.

'Sorry?' was Douro's withering comment. 'These people can't
hear a single word I'm saying.'

'Very, very sorry,' I said again, and again the scornful echo:
'Sorry?' Douro was now walking haughtily back to his party and
then, half-way, turned to have his final word:

'Some people', and he made it clear he was addressing the
visitors as well as myself, 'some people, I have noticed, can *never*
play the organ without letting all bedlam loose.'

When I last paid a visit to St Peter Mancroft, it was to hear
Messiah given as a prelude to the Quincentenary Festival there. I
sat at the extreme west end of the church, and as my eye travelled
the length of the splendid hammer-beam roof with its beautiful
vaulting, I began to wonder what the effect of the recent improve-
ments would have upon Douro Potter, and the Vicar of that period,
Canon F. J. Meyrick. If they could see it now, the spring-clean
look of the stone, I think, would meet with their approval, for in
their time it was so grimy that you didn't fully realize the building's
grand proportions; and as I listened to the organ again I was sure
they would both be gratified by the undertaking, not yet complete,
to restore the instrument.

But there was one thing I think that neither Canon Meyrick nor
his knowledgeable verger would care for, and that is, the strip
lighting which has been fastened to some of the pillars and which
saturates the interior with that kind of light which permits no
shadows, a relentless, unhallowed light which is neither of day nor
of night, neither of this world nor, let us hope, of the next.

But I must not convey the impression that Canon Meyrick was old-fashioned and ultra-conservative. During the twenty-eight years of his incumbency at St Peter Mancroft, he was, on the contrary, noted for his reforming zeal, his open-mindedness, and, not least, his forthright preaching. His appearance suggested that he was something of a poet, indeed his tumbling hair and the shape of his head, faintly reminded one of Yeats; and this suggestion was borne out in the romantic style of his sermons, which he would deliver with the tones and gestures of an actor. To us who assisted him in those far-off days, Canon Meyrick *was* St Peter Mancroft.

John Wesley, setting down in his diary his impressions after a visit to this great Norwich church, wrote: 'It had a venerable look and, at the same time, surprisingly cheerful.' And that also, as it happens, is a good description of Frederick Meyrick.

Memories of the Old Theatre Royal, Norwich *

I never visit the present Theatre Royal at Norwich without attempting to conjure up the magic nights I spent there as a boy in the early years of the century. It is not easy to recapture the feeling of the place. The façade of the present building and its entrance do not suggest that you are about to walk into an enchanted world, as did the entrance to the old Theatre Royal. Gilded embellishments have given place to plain surfaces and austere lines. The pungent aroma of oranges and pears—'like a little glass of wine' we were assured by those who sold them—has been defeated by the smell of fancy disinfectants. Today I enter the Norwich Theatre Royal and think only of the play or opera or whatever it may be I have come to see. In boyhood years, the building itself, its ornament, its smells, its red plush, its acute discomforts, were part of the experience.

When I first knew it, the building was about seventy-five years old. It had been opened on Easter Monday 1826, when a stock company gave *The School for Scandal* and a play called *Youth, Love and Folly* or *The Female Jockey*. The proceeds of the first performance were 'for the relief of the unemployed poor'. A week before the theatre opened, the manager advertised his plans in the *Norwich Mercury* in these words: 'The manager has the honour of announcing to the public that the mode of admission to every part of the theatre will in future be conducted by tickets only, to be

K

purchased from Eleven till Two of Miss Tubby at the Box Office;
and each Evening of performing, the Office for the Sale of Tickets
both for the First and Second Account, will be opened at Five of
the clock.'

Doors were opened at five-thirty for the six o'clock performance.
The prices were 4s. for the Dress Circle, 3s. for the Upper Circle,
2s. the Pit, and 1s. the Gallery. Half-price at half-time. During
the opening performance, according to the *Norwich Mercury*, two
or three 'regular blockheads' kept up a continuous uproar and
'committed a cowardly assault upon the peaceable individual who
vends refreshments'. The *Mercury* was so indignant that it advised
the audience, if such a thing happened again, 'to take the redress
in their own hands'.

The Norwich audience had become more civilized when I first
became one of their number, though voices from the gallery made
their requests heard in no modest manner, especially in demanding
an encore of the Soldiers' Chorus in *Faust*, or 'Turn on, old Time',
in *Maritana*. Even the Dagger Speech was sometimes encored
and Macbeth, having worked himself up to murder point and
entered Duncan's chamber, would sheepishly return and start
the nightmare all over again.

This last incident would be during one of the visits of the F. R.
Benson Company, which, with the annual visit of the Moody-
Manners Opera Company, would almost make up the yearly sum
of my theatre experiences in those days. I could not have been
more than seven years old when I heard my first opera and saw
my first Shakespeare play. I do not know which was the greater
excitement in anticipation, or which, in experience, was the more
golden moment of time.

Perhaps you will recall that travelling Shakespearean Company
of F. R. Benson; if so, I think you will agree with me when I
say that to us these players of fifty years ago were gods and god-
desses, even though few of them were known to the London
public.

Foremost among these super-humans was Henry Herbert.
Every part that he played was coloured by that nasal, melancholy
voice of his.

'Let me tell you, Cassius, you yourself are much condemned' [1]
—that is more or less the sound of it—but nothing could persuade

---

[1] This line intoned as H. H. would have spoken it.

me that he was less than superlative in them all. Hamlet one night, Petruchio the next, Henry the Fifth at the matinée, Malvolio in the evening, Caliban on Saturday afternoon and to wind up the week, Brutus. Each, unmistakably, was Henry Herbert, yet each portrayal had a separate glamour. Occasionally there would be tentative murmurs that perhaps his Romeo was rather hang-dog, perhaps not *quite* the complete illusion, but, in our star-crossed loyalty, we would hastily qualify this by saying that, perhaps with a Juliet other than that of Dorothy Green or Gladys Vanderzee, his Romeo would be the bull's-eye we all wanted it to be.

How we revered this actor! His very walk across the stage would cause us to make strange, half-suppressed noises of admiration—Ah! or Mmm!—as we sat there on the hard, backless benches of the gallery. He it was who, for many of us, removed the stigma of Verity's footnotes, which in the school editions of Shakespeare had defaced every play of Shakespeare that we had unwillingly studied. So uninviting were those school Shakespeare editions, that many plays were left unread, even in the enthusiastic years, and when, in my twenties, John Masefield asked me to take a rehearsal of his village players in *A Winter's Tale*, I was mortified to discover that I knew nothing about the play.

Shakespeare at the old Theatre Royal of Norwich, and especially that one player, Henry Herbert, was responsible for the fever that possessed me for many years after. With a friend I formed a sort of repertory company, a juvenile Shakespearean troupe. How airily we sailed over the frontiers will be realized when I say that within a few months we had rehearsed and produced scenes from *Twelfth Night*, *Julius Caesar*, *Macbeth*, and *The Tempest*. One of our all-male company reached the height of ambition by playing Lady Macbeth after a preliminary canter as Mark Antony.

Our presentation of the murder of Duncan became so famous in the city that we were always in request to help the funds of churches and chapels. We were on tour. Our little company went all round Norwich and the neighbouring country with the bold conviction that we were doing the author of the plays some service. Alas for ideals! Not yet was the heavy ground ready for such tender seed. In some places we did our author harm. For one performance of 'The Murder of Duncan' the audience consisted chiefly of mothers and their young children. Macbeth, which was my particular part, decided that evening to make the scene more picturesque by holding up his hands after the murder so that Duncan's blood might drip from them. There was a panic. And since the only exit from the building was through a door at the back of the improvised platform on which we were acting, the stage was swiftly invaded by screaming children and their angry mothers. Macbeth was no less panic-stricken. 'How is't with me,' he began, 'when every noise appals me?' Then, face to face with an angry mother, telling him he ought to be ashamed, he whispered a few words, which were not in the script, begging the good woman to be reasonable. Reasonable! No one was reasonable that evening. We expected to be thanked at the end by the chapel minister whose funds we were assisting. Instead, he told us we were a disgrace for turning his vestry into a common theatre dressing-room.

If zeal is a saving virtue, we of this little Shakespearean Company were good in our parts, I do believe. We had the confessed ambition to be invited to appear, perhaps in a charity matinée, at the Theatre Royal. To have walked the very boards upon which Henry Herbert had so commandingly prowled—that would have set the seal upon our audacious adventure. But—the invitation never came.

I do not know why cricket and meat pies should be so closely related in my mind except that many years ago, on the Lakenham Ground in Norwich, I used, as a boy, to watch the August-week cricket and, during the lunch interval, used to divide my time between filling up the score-card and devouring the couple of pies I had bought at a well-known bakery in the city, which, by the way, still exists. For a similar reason of associated ideas, Opera has never seemed so grand as when it is heard in early autumn; for, in my boyhood, the annual visit of the Moody-Manners Opera Company to this same Theatre Royal of Norwich, usually coincided with the last weeks of September or the first of October. The wooden benches of the gallery accommodated few people, and, in order to find a place in the front row, I was always one of the first in the queue.

In later years, when I was staying with Elgar at his Worcester home, I told him of some of these early delights, and he in turn told me about the visits of the Haig-Dyer Company to Worcester when *he* was a boy. With great affection he spoke of that brave little band of singers and players who enabled him to make his first acquaintance with *La Traviata, Il Trovatore, Faust,* and *Norma.* I can speak of the Moody-Manners Company with the same affection, and, in doing so, I should like to pay tribute to all such touring organizations in this country for their courageous spirit of enterprise. So long as they could half fill the theatres on their route, Charles Manners and his little group of singers were given heart to continue.

In the confidence of man's estate I have sometimes heard myself saying that, rather than give an opera inadequately it is better not to perform it at all. I would not have said so as a boy—even if I had realized how inadequate some of those performances were.

Almost equal to the pleasure of the opera itself was the excitement of anticipation which ran over us in waves as we stood there in the gallery queue. For good humour, good fellowship, and for stories, there was nothing quite like that queue. It was a friendly club. Suddenly there would be the sound we had all been listening for—the exaggerated clatter of door-bolts being pulled back and the doors being thrown open. Then the surging rush up the stairs, the livelier ones pushing past the others and running past the box-office in the hope of being able to keep a seat for a friend. Then the arranging of one's coat for a cushion, the excited talk, the calling for programmes, the heat, laden with the smell of orange-peel, the puffing and blowing and fanning with handkerchiefs and programmes. Then the leaning over the front-rail as the oboe sounded his A amid the first faint sounds of the orchestra tuning. Then the applause when the conductor appeared—all rather distant, deep-down, and mysterious, that applause—as though we in the gallery had no proper right to be joining in. Then the most exciting moment of all, when your heart was liable to miss a beat—the dimming of the lights, the mystery of the music stirring to life, and then, for an hour or so, we were not there at all. We were lost.

It was all a dream. Yes, in spite of the strange things that used to happen. And some *very* queer things did happen. An exceptional moment of excitement was always the flashing firework which announced the first entry of Mephistopheles in *Faust* (in Norwich, Gounod's opera was always known as 'Forst'.) But on one sad occasion the firework was missing and Mephistopheles entered, unheralded, in the dark. 'Disaster!' we thought, we who were in the know. But Mephistopheles (it may have been William Anderson or perhaps Charles Manners himself) had not sung more than a phrase or two before the firework put in a late appearance, just above his head, and nearly choked him with smoke. The rest of the scene was a mixture of singing and coughing.

Then there was the performance (by an Italian Company this time) of *Rigoletto* when, in the last act, a stage tree fell and landed on Rigoletto's back and put an abrupt end to his passionate out-pouring. There was no way out but for a couple of scene-shifters to come on in their shirt-sleeves and hold up the tree for the rest of the scene.

Without saying it in so many words, my parents always let it be understood that, except for Shakespeare and Grand Opera, the theatre was no place for a boy of my tender years. But of those two exceptions I was permitted to take my fill; and it is interesting to note that, of the many operas I heard at the old Theatre Royal in those days, there are quite a few that I've never heard again; for example, *Maritana, The Bohemian Girl*, and *The Lily of Killarney* were once upon a time all firmly established in the repertory of a travelling company, but, for one reason and another, have since dropped out. For *Maritana* with its succession of easy, pleasant airs (like 'Turn on, old Time') I had great affection, but I always thought that, after the charming duet 'The Moon hath raised', *The Lily of Killarney* seemed to peter out. These de-lightful melodies, I must make clear, were well known to me before I ever saw the operas. My father and his friends were always singing them at home, and I was required to play the accompaniments. From the age of eight, opera and oratorio formed a liberal part of my very liberal education.

On rare occasions, in the name of liberality, I was taken to see a play 'with a moral', but only on condition that I took the lesson to heart. At the old Theatre I saw *The Passing of the Third Floor Back*, but oh! how I longed for the flow and the euphony of a noble or an angry Shakespearean speech, or for such a suddenly flowering moment as the tenor-baritone-bass trio in *Faust*. The only compensation was the *entr'acte* music, an eccentric per-formance by piano, a rather sour and wayward violin, Mr Palmer's amateur flute (Mr Palmer was by trade a clock-mender), and a trumpet which occasionally, and for no very clear reason, blared out a beery bit of melody. The play itself struck me as more oppressive than the dreariest of sermons.

Some years later, I was often a member of another friendly club, the Covent Garden gallery queue. By this means I added greatly to my already rich store of opera memories. If I were asked which of these later memories was outstanding, I think I would not choose my first hearing of McCormack or Destinn or Dinh Gilly, not even the night of Melba's farewell, indestructible though these echoes are, but the occasion when *Prince Igor* was given with the title-role sung in German, another in French, other parts in Russian, while the chorus, I dare say, were singing in Esperanto —all very international and friendly. But not even this bright occasion can eclipse the memory of those nights when the conductor's stick tapped on the stand at the old Norwich Theatre Royal, to tell us to hold our breath and get ready for the sinister green light and the creeping opening chords of *Faust* according to Gounod.

The Critic and His Words

I remember hearing a Cambridge professor, during a series of broadcast talks on the problems of our native language, confess himself defeated by the bewildering changes in present-day English, both written and spoken. Many who are sensitive to language and to words have the same feeling of defeat as they listen to broadcast talks or read the reports of speeches. In an early poem, T. S. Eliot speaks of the continual failure of the would-be master of words, but this present frustration goes deeper than that. It is a feeling that numbers of public speakers and writers no longer have a sense of responsibility towards the English word. They delight in twisting it, turning it upside down, inside out, torturing it.

Defeated for the moment we may be, but we must not be humiliated. Those who are deeply concerned about the preserving of the beauty and dignity of the English language must not be intimidated by the atrocities of speech which are now a daily experience. Whenever we can, we must show that we refuse to condone these ugly practices.

We must protest in fact. Against what, for instance? An exhaustive list of abuses is not my present purpose, but here are a few which are helping to make life hideous. Without being condemned as either pedantic or puristic, we may surely protest against the growing use of nouns as adjectives, of proper names as adjectives (a Churchill riposte, a Hutton drive, a Brahms symphony and, ugliest jargon of all, the Brahms), and of nouns as verbs (I'll contact the Electricity Board).

Before it is too late, let us also protest against the plethora of unnecessary prepositions which we have tolerated too long. Why must we face up to things which formerly we faced? Why must we watch out when all we need do is to watch? When we fall, by what unwritten law do we fall down on? (Is it not the compulsion of some inferior vogue-worship?) Why must a doctor invariably and interminably be writing out prescriptions when it would be so much more graceful merely to be writing them?

These are suggestions, a few only. Everyone who is alive to the natural strength of the English language will have his own aversions. One will want to stress the importance of lifting the increasing burden of compound words from our accommodating vocabulary. An American professor has recently pointed out this danger. Even he, and he should know. Another will think it important to guard against the neuter possessive. Such a one was 'Father' Robin Legge, who when he was Editor of Music for the *Daily Telegraph* used to impress upon me as one of his critics that I must never write of 'last night's concert' or 'Monday's sunshine'. His notion was that inanimate nouns could not possess.

The aversions vary, but as long as there are people who feel them strongly, we need not give way to the feeling which sometimes overtakes us that the English language is slipping from us. It *will* slip from us if we allow ourselves to be bluffed by the debilitated phrases used by those who would like to give an air of being business-like, important, and knowledgeable. But when we bring to mind the great tradition of the English tongue, we take heart. The beauty of a language is not confined to its actual sounds. Other elements play a part, the relation of sound and mood, the expression of thought in terms of rhythm, the interaction of style and matter, and the apt interpretation of ideas by imagery.

A study of representative English writers and speakers, both past and present, always deepens the conviction that the mingling of these elements makes possible a remarkable variety of method and is continually productive of vitality and creative energy. In the hands not only of the master but also of the plain man, English can be a rhapsody, an artillery or an alms-basket. In the hands of those who think and utter in terms of jargon, it all too often becomes a barren superfluity of words.

A Note on Choral and Sociable Music

There is a chapter in Reginald Nettel's *The Englishman Makes Music* which gives an account of Sarah Ann Glover and her Norwich Sol-fa Ladder. With her sisters, Miss Glover kept a girls' day-school in the Black Boy Yard, Colegate Street, Norwich, and with the solfeggio scale painted on a board, contrived in the 1840s to teach her pupils to sing at sight, in time and in tune. She taught better than she knew. Visitors were attracted to the school by reports of Miss Glover's methods. One of them was John Curwen, a Congregational minister, who was interested in the various methods of teaching nonconformist communities to sing. He decided that Miss Glover's was the best for his purpose and, with some small modifications, adapted it.

Tonic sol-fa, that is to say, really began in Colegate, Norwich. The famous system was outlined in a *Grammar of Vocal Music* which John Curwen published in 1843. The story should be an encouragement to every teacher of music. The name of Sarah Ann Glover is now honoured with an entry in Grove's *Dictionary*. But she was not to know that she was making an important contribution to the history of music. Two motives only sustained her teaching: love of singing, and love of children.

About this time, Hullah published Wilhelm's 'Singing Teaching Method' for English use and in a preface wrote: 'The manufacturing population of Norfolk, in like manner, has shown taste in the cultivation of choral music, and has rendered service in the production of oratorios sung at the festivals for which Norwich has been celebrated.'

That Norfolk should have been so commended for attention to choral singing a century and more ago, may be surprising to those who think of the Norfolk singing voice as an unkind reminder of the prevailing north-east wind, and are forgetful of the doggedness of the native character. That same cultivation of choral music is a hundred times more in evidence, almost fervently so, at the present time, thanks to the manifold activities and incentives of the

Women's Institutes, the competitive festivals and the Rural Music School.

From contemporary magazines and publications, and against a background of diverse studies in music and sociology, Mr Nettel, in the book I have mentioned, has gathered and presented an even more impressive array of curious facts than he did in his earlier study called *The Orchestra in England*. No chapter is more telling, if I may borrow a word from its title, than the one called 'Yorkshire Tells the World', which is an account of the work and influence of that grand choral trainer, Henry Coward. Only once did I meet that rugged man whose life was his choral society. That was at Sheffield when I took part in a performance he conducted and afterwards talked with him at supper in company with a few musical friends. He was then at the end of his career, but there was only one word to describe him—irrepressible. Not the presence of Arthur Bliss, who that evening was being lionized, not his hostess, not even his wife could prevent him breaking into every conversation. He would not be curbed. An attack of hiccups suddenly overtook him but that only increased his determination to have his say. I began to understand how it was he made people sing. Something of the same spirit burns in Herbert Bardgett today. That is why *Messiah* by the Huddersfield Choral is like no other.

And something of that spirit has inspired many another choral tradition in England. The Stoke-on-Trent tradition, for example. The pioneer who founded that movement was James Whewall, born at Kingsley, near Cheadle, a parish church choir-boy and, in early years, a miner. He became a choirmaster at the Wesleyan Chapel, formed a children's choir and went prize-hunting. After an accident in the mines, he started an adult choir, the Talke and District choir, and with it won first place in one of the smaller classes of the Welsh National Eisteddfod. He next aimed at the chief choral event of the Eisteddfod, doubled the number of his singers, called the new choir the North Staffordshire District Choral Society, boldly entered the lists, and in the face of unexpected difficulties, again won first prize. It all reads like the story of the rise of some famous football team. Later came the choir's association with Elgar who invited it to give the first London performance of *Gerontius*.

In a final chapter Mr Nettel, drawing his strands of argument together, remarks that as the needs of a new age enforce a trans-formation of our whole manner of thinking, moral and social and musical ideas all suffer change. He quotes Aldous Huxley's passage about synthetic music, where he describes the sound-track roll playing a trio for hyper-viola, super-cello, and oboe surrogate, filling the air 'with its agreeable languor'. Huxley's prophecy has already been overtaken by *musique concrète*, that nightmarish space-war of sound and din, which on occasions has invaded the cinema and soon, I dare say, will be let loose, through the medium of television, into what used to be called the home.

Against all these invasions and irruptions, can the spirit of the amateur hope to stand? Hitherto the amateur has always been welcome to join the professional—choral societies with professional soloists, amateurs and professionals together in an orchestra—to perform certain works, which in the first place were written with this mixture of forces in mind. But amateurs can find no place in synthetic music. They are ruled out in the name of efficiency and precision.

Sooner or later, however, the issue, now obscured by the chronic materialism of the age, will be forced, and the amorphous thing we call the musical public will then perhaps be split in two, one deciding finally for synthetic music (with its much more than human chorus), the other turning its back on all that uncharted sea of sound and returning to the safe retreat of the music it knows or can learn to know, and, if need be, can learn to sing or play for itself.

The music of history and of present-day composers is surely a large enough world for the most adventurous to range over. Rather than be stampeded into laboratory-music, will not the amateur of the near future tend to withdraw from the sheep-crowd and seek occasion for the practice (either private or in a like-minded smaller group such as choral society or local orchestra) of such talent and knowledge of music as he has? All of us are fast suffering change. No doubt about that. But have we no alternative but to be bludgeoned, in the work-shop, in the theatre and cinema, in the home, by music so mechanized that it is utterly devoid of the human spirit?

With the nineteenth-century growth of the big city, the ex-panding choral society and the mammoth annual *Messiah* became social necessities and musical taste could not but be influenced.

But when the machine age threatens to enforce a materialist conception of music—factory music to increase output—must the musician conform? Will he not rather be compelled to return to the platonic idea that the excellence of music must not be spilled for the pleasure of chance persons?

INDEX